WORLDWIDE IN CYBERSPACE
PUBLISHING FOR THE 21ST CENTURY

THE UNIVERSE IS A DREAM

THE SECRETS OF EXISTENCE REVEALED

ALEXANDER MARCHAND

WRITING, ART, AND LETTERING

Inspired Arts Press

Where Art and Spirit Join

WRITING, ART, AND LETTERING
ALEXANDER MARCHAND

THE UNIVERSE IS A DREAM
Copyright © 2010 Alexander Marchand.

Published by Inspired Arts Press
Worldwide in Cyberspace
www.inspiredartspress.com

First Printing: September 2010
10 9 8 7 6 5 4 3 2

Library of Congress Control Number: 2010911950

Subject Headings: Spiritual Life, Course in Miracles, Graphic Novels, Forgiveness, Metaphysics.

ISBN 10: 0-9829230-0-7
ISBN 13: 978-0-9829230-0-9

TABLE OF CONTENTS

THE THREE READERS

THERE ARE THREE MAIN GROUPS OF READERS WHO WILL READ THIS BOOK. THEREFORE, THIS BOOK IS DESIGNED TO SUIT ALL THREE GROUPS OF READERS. WHICH GROUP ARE YOU IN?

ONE: CLUELESS

READERS WHO DON'T REALLY KNOW WHAT THIS BOOK IS ABOUT, BUT ARE NONETHELESS COMPELLED TO READ IT.

TWO: NEWBIES

READERS WHO BASICALLY ALREADY KNOW WHAT THIS BOOK IS ABOUT, BUT ARE NOT YET VERSED IN THE METAPHYSICS IT ESPOUSES.

THREE: REFRESHERS

READERS WHO ALREADY KNOW WHAT THIS BOOK IS ABOUT AND ARE ALREADY VERSED IN THE METAPHYSICS IT ESPOUSES.

IF YOU ARE IN GROUP ONE OR TWO AND DON'T EVENTUALLY MAKE IT TO GROUP THREE, THEN YOU NEVER REALLY READ THIS BOOK.

RULES FOR READING

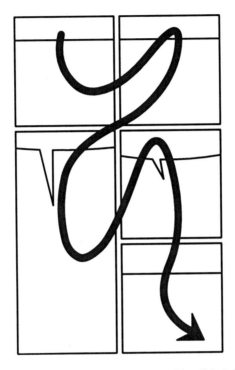

READ FROM LEFT TO RIGHT, UP TO DOWN.

DON'T HESITATE TO REFER TO THE GLOSSARY OF
SYMBOLS (FOUND IN THE BACK OF THE BOOK) WHILE
READING THE BOOK.

READ THE WHOLE BOOK CAREFULLY BEFORE JUMPING TO
CONCLUSIONS.

READ THE BOOK MORE THAN ONCE.

AND REMEMBER TO LAUGH --
EVEN IF YOU DON'T GET THE JOKE.

DEDICATED TO ALL THE DREAMERS
WHO HAVE AND EVER WILL REALIZE
THAT THIS UNIVERSE IS INDEED A
DREAM.

CHAPTER
ZERO

THE BEGINNING OF THE END

-- RIVERRUN, PAST EVE AND ADAM'S...

HI. MY NAME IS **ALEX**.

YOU MAY REMEMBER ME FROM SUCH DREAMS AS --

-- STARTLED BY A GIANT SNAKE --

HEY BABY.

-- UNPREPARED FOR THE FINAL EXAM --

TRUTH & ILLUSION 101

FINAL EXAM
FALL SEMESTER

-- AND THIS BOOK.

YEP, THAT'S RIGHT. THIS BOOK IS A **DREAM**.

YOU DREAMT ME UP TO SEEMINGLY WRITE AND DRAW THIS BOOK FOR YOU.

1

YOU DREAMT ME UP.

YOU DREAMT THIS BOOK UP --

-- YOU DREAMT YOUR LIFE UP --

-- AND YOU DREAMT UP THE ENTIRE UNIVERSE.

DON'T YOU **BELIEVE** ME?

WELL, I ALREADY KNOW THAT YOU DON'T BELIEVE ME. OTHERWISE, YOU'D BE **AWAKE** -- ONLY ILLUSIONS REQUIRE **BELIEF** ANYWAY.

BELIEF PRODUCES THE ACCEPTANCE OF EXISTENCE. THAT IS WHY YOU CAN BELIEVE WHAT NO ONE ELSE THINKS IS TRUE. IT IS **TRUE** FOR YOU BECAUSE IT WAS **MADE** BY YOU.[1]

NOTE: DOTTED CIRCLES LIKE THESE WILL BE USED THROUGHOUT THIS BOOK TO REPRESENT MIND.

YOU SEE, YOU ARE **NOT** A BRAIN OR A BODY; YOU ARE A **MIND**.

MIND

YOU ARE A MIND LOST IN A DREAM OF **DUALITY** -- A DREAM THAT, AS YOU WILL SEE, WAS DREAMT IN OPPOSITION TO NONDUALITY.

BRAINS AND BODIES ARE **UNREAL**; THEY ARE PRODUCTS OF DREAMING; THEY ARE MERE **PUPPETS** DREAMT UP BY THE DREAMING MIND.

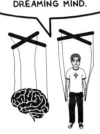

MIND IS THE CREATIVE EXPRESSION OF **SPIRIT**, WHICH, IN ITS PRESENT STATE, IS FOR YOU A **DECISION** MAKER.

AND ALTHOUGH YOU LONG AGO DECIDED TO DREAM, YOU NOW HAVE DECIDED THAT YOU ARE INTERESTED IN WAKING UP.

THAT IS WHY YOU DREAMT ME UP TO MAKE THIS BOOK FOR YOU; IT IS **NO ACCIDENT!**

I AM YOU AS YOU ARE ME AS WE ARE WE AS WE ARE ALL **ONE** MIND. AND THIS BOOK IS HERE TO HELP YOU REALIZE THAT FACT.

GOO GOO G'JOOB

UNLIKE THE **BILLIONS** OF OTHER PIECES OF MEDIA YOU COULD BE CONSUMING RIGHT NOW, YOU HAPPEN TO BE CONSUMING ONE OF THE VERY VERY FEW PIECES OF MEDIA THAT WILL HELP LEAD YOU OUT OF THIS DREAM -- INSTEAD OF DEEPER INTO IT.

UP NEXT
THE UNREAL WORLD
DTV
DOUCHE
LCD   PHONY

SO, CONGRATULATIONS! VERY FEW PEOPLE EVER EVEN GET THAT FAR.

AS THE TITLE OF THIS BOOK STATES, THIS UNIVERSE **IS** A DREAM. AND THIS BOOK IS GOING TO FILL YOU IN ON WHAT YOU'LL NEED TO DO TO **WAKE UP** FROM THIS DREAM UNIVERSE.

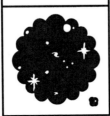

THE FIRST STEP IN WAKING UP IS TO SUSPECT THAT YOU ARE INDEED ASLEEP AND DREAMING.

IS THIS A DREAM?

PLENTY OF PEOPLE THROUGHOUT HISTORY HAVE TAKEN THE FIRST STEP.

FOR EXAMPLE, **BUDDHA** HAD A HANDLE ON THE DREAM QUALITY OF THIS UNIVERSE --

OBJECTS HAVE NO REALITY IN THEMSELVES BUT ARE ONLY SEEN OF THE MIND AND, THEREFORE, ARE OF THE NATURE OF MAYA AND A DREAM.

-- SO DID THE ENGLISH POET AND PLAYWRIGHT PUBLICLY KNOWN AS **WILLIAM SHAKESPEARE** --

WE ARE SUCH STUFF AS DREAMS ARE MADE ON, AND OUR LITTLE LIFE IS ROUNDED WITH A SLEEP.

-- AND THE FRENCH PHILOSOPHER, MATHEMATICIAN, SCIENTIST, AND WRITER **RENÉ DESCARTES** --

WHEN I CONSIDER THIS CAREFULLY, I FIND NOT A SINGLE PROPERTY WHICH WITH CERTAINTY SEPARATES THE WAKING STATE FROM THE DREAM. HOW CAN YOU BE CERTAIN THAT YOUR WHOLE LIFE IS NOT A DREAM?

-- AS WELL AS **MANY** OTHER PEOPLE, BOTH RECORDED IN THE ANNALS OF HISTORY AND UNRECORDED.

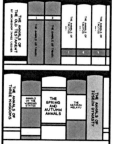

HOWEVER, MERELY SUSPECTING THAT THIS UNIVERSE IS A DREAM IS A **FAR** CRY FROM ACTUALLY GOING ALL THE WAY AND WAKING UP.

HAVE YOU EVER HAD A DREAM THAT YOU WERE SURE WAS REAL? WHAT IF YOU WERE UNABLE TO WAKE FROM THAT DREAM? HOW WOULD YOU KNOW THE DIFFERENCE BETWEEN THE DREAM WORLD AND THE REAL WORLD?

ALEX AS MORPHEUS: THE MATRIX

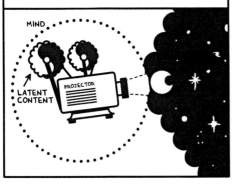

THAT IS BECAUSE THE DOMINANT THOUGHT SYSTEMS OF THIS WORLD ARE BASED ON **DUALISTIC** THINKING.

DUALISTIC THINKING IS THE THINKING OF DREAMS. **NONDUALISTIC** THINKING IS THE THINKING OF WAKING UP.

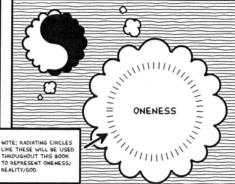

ONENESS

NOTE: RADIATING CIRCLES LIKE THESE WILL BE USED THROUGHOUT THIS BOOK TO REPRESENT ONENESS/ REALITY/GOD.

SO, IF YOU WANT TO WAKE UP, YOU HAVE TO LEARN HOW TO START THINKING NONDUALISTICALLY.

ONLY ONENESS IS.

DREAMS OF DUALITY ARE NOT REALITY. REALITY IS PURELY **NONDUALISTIC**; IT IS PURE ONENESS, WITH NO SEPARATION, NO CONFLICT, NO DIFFERENCES, NO BINARIES.

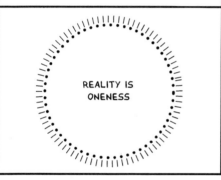

REALITY IS ONENESS

THERE ARE **NO** OPPOSITES IN REALITY; OPPOSITES ONLY SEEMINGLY EXIST IN DREAMS. AS YOU'LL DISCOVER, THAT'S WHAT DIFFERENTIATES REALITY FROM DREAMS.

FROM WITHIN DREAMS, REALITY SEEMS LIKE A DREAM. TO THE DREAMER, THINGS LIKE **GOD**, **HEAVEN**, **INNOCENCE**, AND **ETERNITY** SEEM LIKE FANTASTICAL DREAM IDEAS, WHILE THINGS LIKE INDIVIDUALITY, MATERIALITY, GUILT, AND DEATH SEEM LIKE REALITY.

6

SUCH IS THE PLIGHT OF THE DREAMER. FORTUNATELY FOR YOU THOUGH, THIS BOOK IS HERE TO ACQUAINT YOU WITH INFORMATION FROM BEYOND THIS DREAM -- INFORMATION THAT THE POPULAR YET DEFICIENT THEOLOGIES, PHILOSOPHIES, AND SCIENTIFIC MODELS OF THE WORLD NEVER EVEN SUSPECTED.

HOW DOES THE BRAIN MAKE CONSCIOUSNESS?

IT DOESN'T.

WHY DID GOD CREATE THE UNIVERSE?

GOD DIDN'T.

WHAT IS THE SOURCE OF THE PAIN, UNHAPPINESS, DESTRUCTION, AND CONFLICT IN THIS WORLD?

UNCONSCIOUS GUILT.

WHAT IS THE MEANING OF LIFE?

TO WAKE UP.

PLUS, YOU'LL KNOW WHAT YOU'LL NEED TO DO TO WAKE UP -- YOU'LL KNOW HOW TO **DISSOLVE** THIS DREAM BY PUTTING TO PRACTICE THE POWER OF PURE NONDUALISM.

WHETHER YOU TAKE UP THE CHALLENGE OF WAKING UP OR NOT WILL BE UP TO YOU.

TO DREAM, OR NOT TO DREAM?

THAT IS THE QUESTION.

IF YOU FIND THAT YOU ARE NOT READY, THEN JUST MAKE SURE TO LEAVE IT AT THAT. APPEAL TO THE BETTER **ANGELS** OF YOUR NATURE AND DON'T TRY TO SPOIL IT FOR THE PEOPLE WHO ARE READY.

CHAPTER ONE NINTH

THE SCIENCE OF DREAMING

THE CONQUEST OF NATURE IS TO BE ACHIEVED THROUGH MEASURE AND NUMBER.

THAT IS WHAT AN ANGEL TOLD A YOUNG **RENE DESCARTES** WHILE HE WAS IN ULM, GERMANY DURING THE AUTUMN OF 1619.

THE ANGEL APPEARED TO DESCARTES IN A SERIES OF DREAMS. DESCARTES DESCRIBED THE ANGEL AS THE ANGEL OF **TRUTH**. THE ANGEL EMPHASIZED TO DESCARTES THAT **MATH** WAS THE KEY TO UNLOCKING THE SECRETS OF NATURE.

$$1 - 1\frac{(1-1)}{X} = 1$$

AMONGST OTHER THINGS, DESCARTES WENT ON TO WRITE **DISCOURSE ON THE METHOD**, WHICH HELPED ESTABLISH THE **SCIENTIFIC METHOD**.

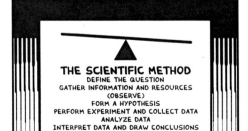

THE SCIENTIFIC METHOD
DEFINE THE QUESTION
GATHER INFORMATION AND RESOURCES (OBSERVE)
FORM A HYPOTHESIS
PERFORM EXPERIMENT AND COLLECT DATA
ANALYZE DATA
INTERPRET DATA AND DRAW CONCLUSIONS
PUBLISH RESULTS
RETEST

SO, ALTHOUGH IT ISN'T OFTEN COVERED IN SCIENCE CLASSES, IT IS HARD TO SAY WHERE THE WORLD WOULD BE TODAY WITHOUT DESCARTES' ANGELIC DREAMING. WOULD THERE HAVE BEEN A **NEWTON** OR AN **EINSTEIN**?

THROUGH THE HELP OF SCIENCE, AND ITS EMPHASIS ON **FALSIFIABLE** HYPOTHESES, WE HAVE CERTAINLY DISCOVERED A LOT ABOUT THIS UNIVERSE OVER THE COURSE OF THE LAST FEW HUNDRED YEARS.

HOWEVER, THE MORE WE HAVE DISCOVERED, THE MORE WE HAVE REALIZED THAT THERE IS STILL MUCH MORE TO DISCOVER.

THAT IS BECAUSE, WHILE UNBEKNOWNST TO SCIENCE, ALL ATTEMPTS AT UNDERSTANDING A DREAM FROM WITHIN A DREAM MUST BE **INCOMPLETE**. OTHERWISE, THE DREAMER WOULD WAKE UP.

IN 1931, AUSTRIAN MATHEMATICIAN **KURT GÖDEL** PUBLISHED SOMETHING CALLED THE INCOMPLETENESS THEOREM.

THE INCOMPLETENESS THEOREM:

ARITHMETIC IS NOT COMPLETELY FORMALIZABLE. FOR EVERY CONSISTENT FORMALIZATION OF ARITHMETIC, THERE EXIST ARITHMETIC TRUTHS THAT ARE NOT PROVABLE WITHIN THAT FORMAL SYSTEM.

GÖDEL'S DISCOVERY WAS QUITE SIGNIFICANT; IT DEMONSTRATED THAT ANY CONSISTENT FORMAL FRAMEWORK USED TO SPEAK ABOUT THE TRUTH OR FALSITY OF MATHEMATICAL STATEMENTS MUST REFERENCE ITSELF, RENDERING IT DOOMED TOO **INCOMPLETENESS**.

A GENERIC FORMAL SYSTEM IN LOGIC SPACE

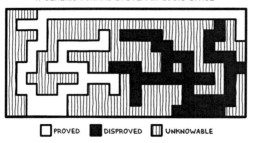

☐ PROVED ■ DISPROVED ▥ UNKNOWABLE

TRANSLATED INTO EVERYDAY APPLICATION, GÖDEL'S INCOMPLETENESS THEOREM LEADS TO THE REALIZATION THAT --

-- WHEN WE TRY TO STUDY THIS UNIVERSE AND SUM IT UP INTO A NICE LITTLE **MODEL**, WHATEVER MODEL WE COME UP WITH MUST BE AT LEAST **SELF-CONTRADICTING** AND MOST LIKELY ALSO DOWNRIGHT **INCOMPLETE**.

THAT MEANS WE'LL NEVER REALLY BE ABLE TO PROVE THE COMPLETE TRUTH OF ANYTHING IN THIS UNIVERSE -- WHICH MAKES PERFECT SENSE SINCE EVERYTHING IN THIS UNIVERSE IS ULTIMATELY A DREAM AND SO UNTRUE.

EVERYTHING IN THIS DREAM IS A LIE...EXCEPT FOR THIS STATEMENT OF COURSE.

THE **UNFACTS**, DID WE POSSESS THEM, ARE TOO IMPRECISELY FEW TO WARRANT OUR **CERTITUDE**.

TO COME UP WITH COMPLETE TRUTH, WE'D HAVE TO STEP **OUTSIDE** THIS UNIVERSE.

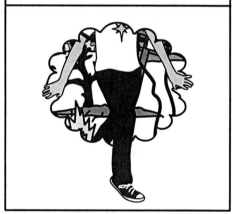

BUT IF WE STEPPED OUTSIDE THIS UNIVERSE, THIS UNIVERSE WOULD **DISAPPEAR** LIKE THE DREAM THAT IT IS BECAUSE WE'D WAKE UP. WE'D FIND OUT THAT THIS UNIVERSE WAS UNTRUE.

BODIES WOULD OF COURSE DISAPPEAR TOO SINCE THEY ARE PART OF THE UNIVERSE.

IF THIS UNIVERSE DIDN'T DISAPPEAR, WE'D STILL BE DREAMING THIS UNIVERSE, BUT FROM A DIFFERENT **POINT OF VIEW**.

WITHIN THIS UNIVERSE, WE ARE STUCK WITH **LIMITED** POINTS OF VIEW.

A POINT OF VIEW IS A BYPRODUCT OF **PERCEPTION**.

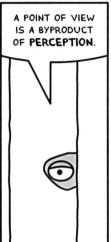

TO PERCEIVE SOMETHING IS TO BE **CONSCIOUS** OF IT.

TO **NOT** PERCEIVE SOMETHING THAT COULD BE PERCEIVED IS TO BE **UNCONSCIOUS** OF IT.

PERCEPTION IS LIMITED BECAUSE IT IS **DUALISTIC** AND DEPENDS ON **ACCEPTING** AND **REJECTING**; IT IS AN ACT OF **JUDGMENT** THAT LEAVES THINGS OUT.

IMAGE ADAPTED FROM MESSAGE D'AMOUR DES DAUPHINS SANDRO DEL-PRETE 1987

14 SMALL DOLPHINS SWIMMING AMONGST CORAL...OR SOMETHING ELSE?

TO PERCEIVE **EVERYTHING** WOULD MEAN THE **ELIMINATION** OF THE **UNCONSCIOUS**; IT WOULD MEAN BEING CONSCIOUS OF EVERYTHING: TOTAL CONSCIOUSNESS.

CONSCIOUSNESS IS LIKE THE TIP OF AN ICEBERG.

UNCONSCIOUSNESS IS LIKE THE PART OF THE ICEBERG HIDDEN UNDERWATER.

THE UNCONSCIOUS

TOTAL CONSCIOUSNESS IS A **TIPPING POINT** THAT LEADS EITHER TO DREAMING OR TO THE END OF PERCEPTION.

CONSCIOUSNESS SYMBOL

THUS, TOTAL CONSCIOUSNESS IS **THE BEGINNING** AND THE **END** OF THIS UNIVERSE.

SCIENTIFIC DISCOVERIES AND OBSERVATIONS OVER THE LAST SEVERAL DECADES HAVE TRACED THE BEGINNING OF THIS UNIVERSE TO THE **BIG BANG**.

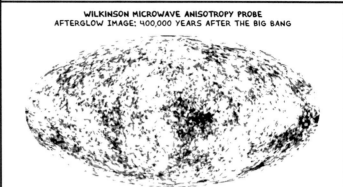

WILKINSON MICROWAVE ANISOTROPY PROBE
AFTERGLOW IMAGE: 400,000 YEARS AFTER THE BIG BANG

THE BIG BANG IS THE COSMOLOGICAL MODEL OF THE INITIAL CONDITIONS OF THIS UNIVERSE, AND OF WHAT TRANSPIRED THEREAFTER.

THE **BIG BANG MODEL** SAYS THAT THIS UNIVERSE STARTED OUT AT A **MICROSCOPIC** SCALE IN A STATE OF EXTREME **DENSITY** AND **HEAT** FROM WHICH IT EXPANDED OUTWARD AND COOLED.

AND THE UNIVERSE CONTINUES TO EXPAND OUTWARD TO THIS DAY -- DUE TO A MYSTERIOUS FORCE CALLED **DARK ENERGY** THAT REPELS THE GRAVITATIONAL TENDENCY FOR EVERYTHING TO COLLAPSE BACK INTO THE MICROSCOPIC SCALE FROM WHICH IT AROSE.

ALL THAT IS PRETTY COOL TO KNOW, BUT IT DOESN'T ANSWER THE QUESTION OF **WHY**.

WHY WAS THERE SEEMINGLY A BIG BANG?

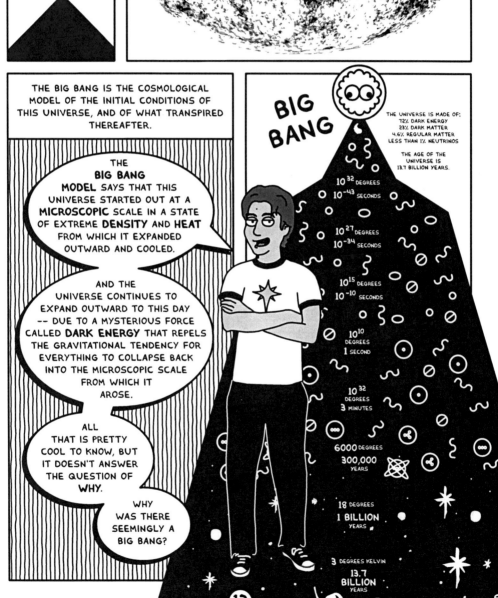

BIG BANG

THE UNIVERSE IS MADE OF:
72% DARK ENERGY
23% DARK MATTER
4.6% REGULAR MATTER
LESS THAN 1% NEUTRINOS

THE AGE OF THE UNIVERSE IS 13.7 BILLION YEARS.

10^{32} DEGREES
10^{-43} SECONDS

10^{27} DEGREES
10^{-34} SECONDS

10^{15} DEGREES
10^{-10} SECONDS

10^{10} DEGREES
1 SECOND

10^{32} DEGREES
3 MINUTES

6000 DEGREES
300,000 YEARS

18 DEGREES
1 BILLION YEARS

3 DEGREES KELVIN
13.7 BILLION YEARS

13

THE WHY QUESTION IS BEYOND THE LIMITATIONS OF SCIENCE. THE WHY QUESTION IS A **PSYCHOLOGICAL** QUESTION AND IT CAN ONLY BE ANSWERED FROM OUTSIDE THE DREAM, BY THE PART OF THE MIND THAT MEDIATES BETWEEN THE DREAMING AND AWAKENED MIND.

IN THIS DREAM UNIVERSE, THE SEEMINGLY PHYSICAL IS MERELY A RESULT OF THE **PSYCHOLOGY** OF THE DREAMER.

FILM = DREAMER'S PSYCHOLOGY

PROJECTOR

PROJECTION = UNIVERSE

THE BIG BANG WAS NOT QUITE THE BEGINNING OF THIS UNIVERSE, **CONSCIOUSNESS** WAS.

10^{32} DEGREES
10^{-43} SECONDS

A LOT OF PEOPLE TRY TO IMBUE CONSCIOUSNESS WITH ALL KINDS OF SPIRITUAL CONNOTATIONS.

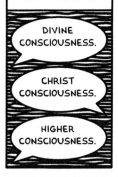

DIVINE CONSCIOUSNESS.

CHRIST CONSCIOUSNESS.

HIGHER CONSCIOUSNESS.

BUT CONSCIOUSNESS IS ULTIMATELY A **DUALISTIC ILLUSION**; IT IS A THING OF DREAMS NOT REALITY.

CONSCIOUSNESS REQUIRES THE DIVISION OF ONE THING INTO **TWO** THINGS: AN OBSERVER AND AN OBSERVED, A SUBJECT AND AN OBJECT.

SUBJECT
(OBSERVER)

OBJECT
(OBSERVED)

CONSCIOUSNESS IS THEREFORE THE ACT OF ENTERTAINING THE CONCEPT OF DUALISTIC **OTHERNESS**; IT IS THE GENESIS OF PERCEPTION.

CONSCIOUSNESS

DUALISM

WHICH MEANS THAT THERE IS NO SUCH THING AS AN **OBJECTIVE OBSERVER.** IN THIS UNIVERSE, THE OBSERVER IS ULTIMATELY THE OBSERVED.

ONE MIND APPEARING AS MANY OBSERVES AND IS OBSERVED.

THE PERCEIVED IS THE PERCEIVER.

THE DREAM IS THE DREAMER.

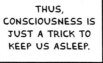

THUS, CONSCIOUSNESS IS JUST A TRICK TO KEEP US ASLEEP.

AND WE FALL FOR IT BECAUSE, AS DREAMERS, WE BELIEVE WE ARE BODIES. CONSEQUENTLY, WE BELIEVE WHAT OUR BODIES DECEPTIVELY TELL US.

BODIES ARE PRODUCTS OF CONSCIOUSNESS. BECAUSE TO PERCEIVE SOMETHING REQUIRES SOMETHING WITH WHICH TO PERCEIVE, AND SOMETHING TO PERCEIVE.

BODIES FULFILL BOTH THOSE REQUIREMENTS.

BODIES COME IN MANY FORMS, BECAUSE IN ORDER FOR BODIES TO PERCEIVE EACH OTHER THEY MUST BE SEEMINGLY DIFFERENT FROM EACH OTHER.

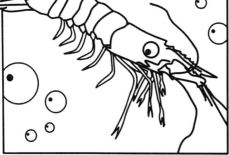

A SIMPLE EXAMPLE OF A BODY IS AN **ELECTRON**. AN ELECTRON PERCEIVES ITS ENVIRONMENT BY DIFFERENTIATING BETWEEN DIFFERENT SUBATOMIC PARTICLES AND REACTING TO THEM ACCORDINGLY.

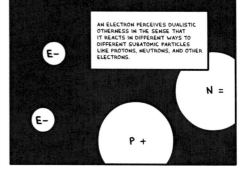

AN ELECTRON PERCEIVES DUALISTIC OTHERNESS IN THE SENSE THAT IT REACTS IN DIFFERENT WAYS TO DIFFERENT SUBATOMIC PARTICLES LIKE PROTONS, NEUTRONS, AND OTHER ELECTRONS.

E−

E−

N =

P +

AN ATOM IS ALSO A BODY.	SO IS A CELL.	SO IS A PLANT.	AND SO IS A PLANET.

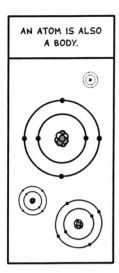 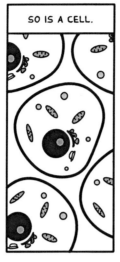  

ALL **THINGS** ARE BODIES OF SOME ORDER. THEY ARE BODIES MADE OF BODIES MADE OF BODIES THAT ARE ULTIMATELY MADE OF **THOUGHT.**

IN THIS DREAM UNIVERSE, ALL BODIES ARE **THOUGHTS**; THEY ARE THOUGHTS OF **SEPARATION**, THOUGHTS OF **DUALISM.** OR, IN OTHER WORDS, THEY ARE PRODUCTS OF CONSCIOUSNESS.

THOUGHT, WHEN PROJECTED OUTWARD, GIVES RISE TO THE **COLLECTIVE HALLUCINATION** THAT WE CALL THE PHYSICAL UNIVERSE.

THEREFORE, PROJECTED THOUGHT IS WHAT WE CALL **ENERGY.**

HIGHLY CONCENTRATED ENERGY IS WHAT MAKES MATTER. THAT IS WHAT EINSTEIN'S EQUATION $E=MC^2$ IS ALL ABOUT.

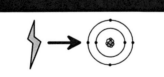

THE ENERGY (E) CONTAINED IN A PIECE OF MATTER EQUALS ITS MASS (M) TIMES THE SPEED OF LIGHT (C) SQUARED.

ENERGY IS THE THOUGHT OF DREAMS; IT **IS ILLUSORY** THOUGHT.

16

THUS, THE SEEMINGLY PHYSICAL LAWS OF THIS UNIVERSE ARE MERELY THE **HABITUAL** THOUGHT PATTERNS OF OUR ONE DREAMING MIND.

THOSE THOUGHT PATTERNS MAKE UP THE SEEMINGLY PHYSICAL WORLD OF BODIES.

AND BODIES IN TURN ACT AS TOOLS FOR EXPERIENTIALLY SHARING CERTAIN **HALLUCINATIONS**.

WHICH IS ANOTHER WAY OF SAYING THAT BODIES HELP **LIMIT** PERCEPTION AND THUS HELP LIMIT COMMUNICATION TO A **FINITE** SET OF CHANNELS.

FOR INSTANCE, A HUMAN EAR CAN ONLY RECEIVE VIBRATIONS WITHIN A FREQUENCY RANGE OF 20 HERTZ TO 20,000 HERTZ.

A HUMAN EYE CAN ONLY RECEIVE ELECTROMAGNETIC RADIATION WITHIN A RANGE CALLED THE **VISIBLE SPECTRUM**.

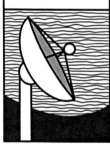

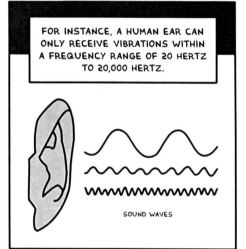

SOUND WAVES

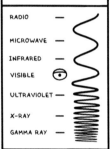

THROUGH INSTRUMENTS THAT ACT AS EXTENSIONS OF THE HUMAN BODY, HUMANS CAN RECEIVE AND THUS PERCEIVE THINGS FAR BEYOND THEIR HABITUAL BODILY LIMITS.

YET, INSTRUMENTS ARE THEMSELVES ALSO ULTIMATELY LIMITED.

NOT ONLY ARE INSTRUMENTS LIMITED IN THE SENSE THAT THEY CAN ONLY SEE A TINY PIECE OF THE WHOLE PUZZLE, BUT THEY ARE ALSO LIMITED IN THE SENSE THAT PEOPLE TEND TO ONLY BUILD INSTRUMENTS TO LOOK FOR AND MEASURE THINGS THAT THEY EXPECT TO FIND.

WHERE IN THE WORLD ARE MY KEYS?

CONSEQUENTLY, THE INFORMATION WE GATHER AND USE AS EVIDENCE TO SUPPORT OUR MODELS OF THIS LITTLE DREAM UNIVERSE OF OURS IS DOOMED TO INCOMPLETENESS.

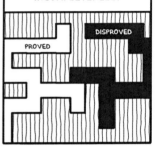

PROVED

DISPROVED

EVIDENCE IS **NOT** PROOF. AND WHEN INCOMPLETE INFORMATION IS ALL WE HAVE TO USE AS EVIDENCE TO SUPPORT OUR MODELS, OUR MODELS ARE BOUND TO BE **INCOMPLETE** AND VULNERABLE TO FALSIFICATION.

FOR INSTANCE, THERE WAS ONCE PLENTY OF EVIDENCE SUGGESTING THAT THE SUN REVOLVES AROUND THE EARTH. WE KNOW DIFFERENTLY NOW THANKS TO ADDITIONAL INFORMATION.

AND THERE IS NO REASON TO THINK THAT MANY POPULAR SCIENTIFIC IDEAS OF TODAY WON'T MEET THAT SAME FATE UPON THE DISCOVERY OF FURTHER INFORMATION.

TAKE THE IDEA THAT HUMANS ARE **EVOLUTIONARY** RELATIVES OF APES AS AN EXAMPLE.

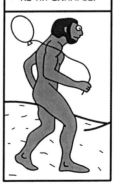

WHO KNOWS? HUMAN ORIGINS COULD BE MUCH STRANGER THAN THE PRESENT **APE CONSENSUS** PROPOSES.

18

FOR INSTANCE, HUMAN ORIGINS COULD BE **EXTRATERRESTRIAL** -- MEANING THAT HUMANS COULD BE ALIENS OF SOME KIND. CONSEQUENTLY, THERE COULD BE COMPELLING EVIDENCE JUST WAITING TO BE UNEARTHED LINKING HUMANS TO ALIENS --

-- WHICH WOULD RENDER THE OLD SHARED EVOLUTIONARY ANCESTRY WITH **APES** MODEL FALSIFIED, AND THUS QUITE **LAME** QUITE QUICKLY.

AND IF THAT HAPPENED, THEN THE OLD EVIDENCE LINKING HUMANS TO APES, LIKE THE SIMILARITY BETWEEN APE DNA AND HUMAN DNA, WOULD NEED TO BE REINTERPRETED.

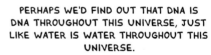

PERHAPS WE'D FIND OUT THAT DNA IS DNA THROUGHOUT THIS UNIVERSE, JUST LIKE WATER IS WATER THROUGHOUT THIS UNIVERSE.

THEREFORE, IT WOULD BE EXPECTED THAT TWO SIMILAR TYPES OF WARM-BLOODED, BIPEDAL ANIMAL BODIES ADAPTED TO THE SAME PLANETARY ENVIRONMENT WOULD HAVE SIMILAR DNA REGARDLESS OF THEIR SO-CALLED TERRESTRIAL ORIGINS.

WE'D REALIZE THAT WHEREVER CONDITIONS ARE FIT THROUGHOUT THIS UNIVERSE FOR BIOLOGICAL LIFE, DNA RENDERS THE SAME KINDS OF BODIES BECAUSE DNA IS DNA AND ORGANIZES IN A CONSISTENT MANNER.

NONETHELESS, WHETHER HUMAN BODIES CAME FROM APES, ALIENS, BOTH, OR SOMETHING ELSE, THEY ALWAYS WERE AND STILL ARE MERELY **PUPPETS** IN A DREAM.

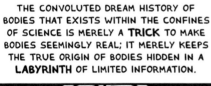

BECAUSE THE TRUE ORIGIN OF BODIES IS OUR DREAMING MIND.

THE CONVOLUTED DREAM HISTORY OF BODIES THAT EXISTS WITHIN THE CONFINES OF SCIENCE IS MERELY A **TRICK** TO MAKE BODIES SEEMINGLY REAL; IT MERELY KEEPS THE TRUE ORIGIN OF BODIES HIDDEN IN A **LABYRINTH** OF LIMITED INFORMATION.

SCIENCE IS A SYSTEM FOR MAKING **FALSIFIABLE METAPHORS** THAT SOMETIMES PROVE USEFUL IN THE CONSTRUCTION OF TOOLS FOR **MODIFYING**, **EXTENDING**, AND **PACIFYING** BODIES.

PENICILLIN

THAT MAKES SCIENCE HANDY WITHIN THIS DREAM, BUT IT DOESN'T MAKE SCIENCE THE ULTIMATE **ARBITER** OF TRUTH -- WHICH IS WHAT PEOPLE TOO OFTEN TRY TO MISUSE IT AS.

SCIENCE SEARCHES FOR TRUTH BY STUDYING A VAST **ILLUSION**.

IT ASKS BODIES, WHICH WERE MADE TO HIDE REALITY, TO TELL US WHAT REALITY IS.

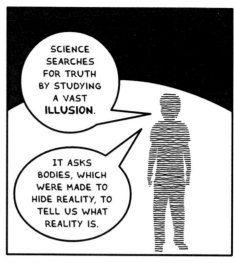

SO, GIVEN THAT PREMISE, IT SHOULD COME AS NO SURPRISE THAT SCIENCE IS AUTOMATICALLY DOOMED TO FAILURE.

TRUTH IS **WITHIN** NOT WITHOUT.

ONENESS IS THE ONLY THING THAT CAN TRULY BE KNOWN.

NONETHELESS, FOR PEOPLE WILLING TO TAKE THINGS TO THEIR LOGICAL CONCLUSION, SCIENCE IS PERFECTLY CAPABLE OF PROVIDING PLENTY OF HELPFUL **EVIDENCE** SUGGESTING THAT THIS UNIVERSE IS INDEED AN **UNREAL DREAM** -- JUST LOOK AT **QUANTUM PHYSICS** AS A PRIME EXAMPLE.

AMONGST OTHER THINGS, **QUANTUM PHYSICS** HAS SHOWN THAT --

-- THE ACT OF OBSERVATION ALTERS OBSERVED PHENOMENON --

-- AND THAT ALL THINGS ARE CONNECTED AT THE QUANTUM LEVEL: UNIMPEDED BY SPACETIME.

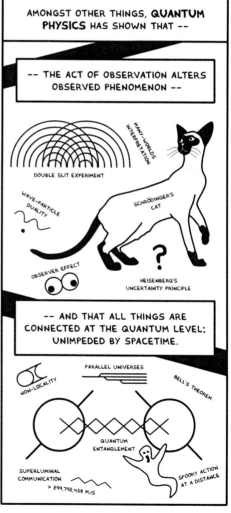

NOW, OF COURSE, NOT ALL PEOPLE ARE WILLING TO ACCEPT THE FULL IMPLICATIONS OF THOSE DISCOVERIES.

BUT THAT IS SIMPLY BECAUSE, AS DREAMERS, WE TAUGHT THE WORLD TO TEACH US ONLY WHAT WE WANTED TO LEARN. WE SET IT ALL UP.

SO, WE ALL FIND AND INTERPRET THIS UNIVERSE ACCORDING TO OUR OBJECTIVE: CONTINUED SLEEP OR AWAKENING.

NONETHELESS, WE WILL ALL EVENTUALLY DISCOVER THAT --

-- THE **UNTRUTH** OF THIS UNIVERSE IS THIS UNIVERSE'S ONLY TRUTH.

THE SOCIAL HIERARCHY OF TRUTH

NUMBER OF BELIEVERS	LABEL OF THE BELIEF
1 PERSON	A DELUSION
A SMALL GROUP	A CULT
A MEDIUM TO LARGE GROUP	A RELIGION, PHILOSOPHY, OR **CULTURE**
A REGION	A GOVERNMENT
MOST PEOPLE	THE TRUTH

WHICH IS A TRICKY CONCEPT SINCE, FROM OUR PERSPECTIVE AS DREAMERS, THIS UNIVERSE SEEMS REAL. THEREFORE, THE TRUTH THAT THIS UNIVERSE IS UNTRUE IS SEEMINGLY SELF-CONTRADICTING.

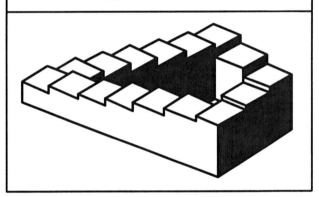

BUT THAT SEEMING SELF-CONTRADICTION IS SIMPLY DUE TO THE FACT THAT TRUTH FROM WITHIN THIS UNIVERSE IS LIMITED.

THE ONLY THING THAT IS UNLIMITED IN THIS UNIVERSE IS THE MIND THAT DREAMT UP THE IDEA OF LIMITATIONS BY DREAMING UP DUALITY, WHICH --

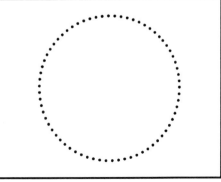

-- MADE MIND A PERCEIVER INSTEAD OF A CREATOR.

IN DREAMS, MIND **PERCEIVES**; IN REALITY, MIND **CREATES**.

WHAT WE CALL CREATION IN THIS UNIVERSE IS **DUALISTIC MAKING**.

WHEN WE **MAKE** THINGS IN THIS UNIVERSE, THEY ARE SEEMINGLY **SEPARATE** FROM US, **IMPERMANENT**, AND **DIFFERENT**. THAT IS BY NO MEANS TRUE CREATION.

TRUE CREATION [VERSUS] DUALISTIC MAKING

TRUE CREATION IS NONDUALISTIC.

TRUE CREATION IS TRUE GIVING. IT EXTENDS THE LIMITLESS TO THE UNLIMITED, ETERNITY TO TIMELESSNESS, AND LOVE UNTO ITSELF. IT ADDS TO ALL THAT IS COMPLETE ALREADY, NOT IN SIMPLE TERMS OF ADDING MORE, FOR THAT IMPLIES THAT IT WAS LESS BEFORE. IT ADDS BY LETTING WHAT CANNOT CONTAIN ITSELF FULFILL ITS AIM OF GIVING EVERYTHING IT HAS AWAY, SECURING IT FOREVER FOR ITSELF. [1]

IN THAT SENSE, TRUE CREATION IS **QUALITATIVE**; IT IS ABOUT QUALITY, NOT QUANTITY.

MAKING ON THE OTHER HAND IS DUALISTIC.

MAKING IS TAKING. IT PROJECTS THE LIMITLESS TO LIMIT, ETERNITY TO TIME, AND LOVE UNTO OTHERNESS. IT ADDS TO COMPENSATE LACK BY STEALING FROM ANOTHER. THUS, IT ADDS BY EMPHASIZING DIFFERENCE AND INDIVI**DUALITY**, TAKING FROM THE WHOLE TO MAKE THAT WHICH IS LESS THAN EVERYTHING AND SEPARATE FROM ITS MAKER.

IN THAT SENSE, MAKING IS **QUANTITATIVE**; THROUGH DIVISION FROM WHOLENESS, IT IS LESS THAN AND DIFFERENT FROM THE WHOLE IN A QUANTITATIVE MANNER.

DID YOU GET ALL THAT?

DON'T WORRY, IF YOU ALREADY UNDERSTOOD ALL THE CONCEPTS IN THIS BOOK, YOU WOULDN'T NEED THIS BOOK.

WE'LL PICK UP ON CONCEPTS MENTIONED IN THIS CHAPTER IN NUMEROUS WAYS AS WE PROCEED THROUGH THIS BOOK.

CONSEQUENTLY, THESE IDEAS WILL BEGIN TO FIT TOGETHER AND MAKE MORE SENSE.

SO, BE **PATIENT**.

FOR NOW, JUST REALIZE THAT THIS UNIVERSE IS A **DREAM**. THERE IS ONE DREAM AND ONE MIND DOING THE DREAMING, BUT WE EXPERIENCE THE DREAM FROM LIMITED VIEWPOINTS THAT FACILITATE THE ILLUSION OF OUR INDIVIDUAL EXISTENCES AND INDIVIDUAL MINDS.

PROJECTOR

THE FACT IS, THIS UNIVERSE HAS NO REALITY OTHER THAN YOUR **BELIEF** IN IT.

THIS UNIVERSE IS **IMPOSSIBLE**. THAT IS WHY IT IS A DREAM.

THANK **GOD**!

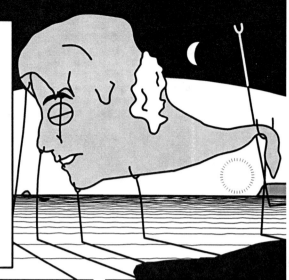

CHAPTER
TWO NINTHS

THE PRODIGAL DREAMER

HAVE YOU EVER HEARD OF THE MASTER PSYCHOLOGIST NAMED **Y'SHUA**?

HE'S THE **MIND** WHO GAVE ME THE IDEAS TO PUT TOGETHER THIS BOOK --

-- I'LL EXPLAIN WHAT THAT MEANS NEAR THE END OF THIS BOOK.

Y'SHUA OR **YESHUA**, PRONOUNCED WITH AN EMPHASIS ON THE SECOND SYLLABLE, WAS THE ACTUAL NAME OF **JESUS**.

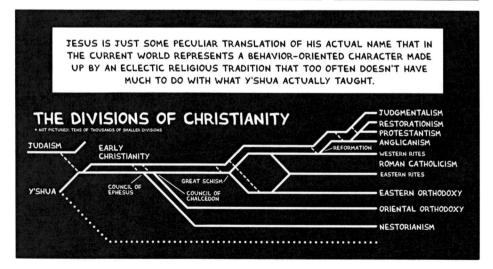

JESUS IS JUST SOME PECULIAR TRANSLATION OF HIS ACTUAL NAME THAT IN THE CURRENT WORLD REPRESENTS A BEHAVIOR-ORIENTED CHARACTER MADE UP BY AN ECLECTIC RELIGIOUS TRADITION THAT TOO OFTEN DOESN'T HAVE MUCH TO DO WITH WHAT Y'SHUA ACTUALLY TAUGHT.

THE DIVISIONS OF CHRISTIANITY
* NOT PICTURED: TENS OF THOUSANDS OF SMALLER DIVISIONS

JUDAISM

EARLY CHRISTIANITY

Y'SHUA

COUNCIL OF EPHESUS

GREAT SCHISM

COUNCIL OF CHALCEDON

REFORMATION

JUDGMENTALISM
RESTORATIONISM
PROTESTANTISM
ANGLICANISM
WESTERN RITES
ROMAN CATHOLICISM
EASTERN RITES

EASTERN ORTHODOXY

ORIENTAL ORTHODOXY

NESTORIANISM

SO, WHETHER YOU ARE A FAN OF JESUS OR HAVE AN AVERSION TO JESUS, IT DOESN'T MATTER. IN THIS BOOK, I'M GOING TO BE TALKING ABOUT Y'SHUA.

Y'SHUA WAS A MIND WHO MANAGED TO WAKE UP.

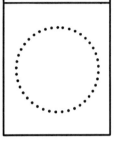

HE WOKE UP TO HIS TRUE IDENTITY, WHICH, IN CHRISTIAN TERMINOLOGY, IS REPRESENTED BY THE WORD **CHRIST**.

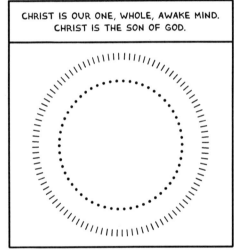

CHRIST IS OUR ONE, WHOLE, AWAKE MIND. CHRIST IS THE SON OF GOD.

Y'SHUA WAS NO MORE OR LESS THE SON OF GOD THAN YOU, ME, OR ANYONE ELSE, INCLUDING ANIMALS AND ROCKS.

SO, CRAZY PEOPLE WHO GO AROUND CLAIMING TO BE JESUS AREN'T AS FAR OFF AS THEY MAY SEEM.

I AM THE SECOND COMING OF JESUS. I NEED MONEY FOR KUNG FU LESSONS TO DEFEAT THE ANTICHRIST.

Y'SHUA HAD A NEAT LITTLE STORY HE USED TO TELL PEOPLE CALLED THE PRODIGAL SON -- ALSO KNOWN AS THE LOST SON.

SUMMED UP, THE STORY WENT LIKE THIS:

THERE WAS ONCE A FATHER WITH TWO SONS.

THE YOUNGEST SON ONE DAY ASKED HIS FATHER IF HE COULD COLLECT HIS **INHERITANCE**.

THE FATHER GAVE THE SON HIS INHERITANCE AND THE SON **LEFT HOME** TO MAKE HIS **OWN LIFE**.

ADIOS POPS!

THE SON SPENT HIS MONEY **FOOLISHLY** AND SOON FOUND HIMSELF **BROKE** AND IN A STATE OF **LACK**.

DRINKS ARE ON ME!

GET OUT OF HERE...YOU BROKE BUM!

HOWEVER, THE SON WAS **AFRAID** TO RETURN TO HIS FATHER BECAUSE HE FEARED HIS FATHER MIGHT **PUNISH** HIM FOR LEAVING HOME AND SQUANDERING HIS INHERITANCE.

YOU REALLY BLEW IT KID.

AND THAT IS JUST TOUGH, YOU MADE YOUR CHOICE.

NOW GET THE HELL OUT OF HERE!

SO, AS A SUBSTITUTE, THE SON FORGED A **SPECIAL RELATIONSHIP** WITH A PERSON WHO GAVE HIM A JOB FEEDING PIGS.

AFTER AWHILE -- EVEN THOUGH THE SON WAS STILL FEELING **GUILTY** FOR LEAVING AND SO **FEARED** HIS FATHER'S **RETRIBUTION** -- THE SON FINALLY DECIDED TO **RETURN HOME**.

I'M BACK.

WHEN HE RETURNED HOME, HIS FATHER WELCOMED HIM BACK WITH OPEN ARMS AND CELEBRATED AS IF **NOTHING** HAD EVER HAPPENED.

SON, THOU ART EVER WITH ME, AND ALL THAT I HAVE IS THINE. IT WAS MEET THAT WE SHOULD MAKE MERRY, AND BE GLAD --

-- FOR THIS THY BROTHER WAS DEAD, AND IS ALIVE AGAIN; AND WAS LOST, AND IS FOUND.

THE **END**... THE BEGINNING.

THAT STORY IS AN **ALLEGORY** FOR THE DREAMING OF THIS UNIVERSE.

IT IS NOT LITERAL!

THE FATHER REPRESENTS **GOD**. WE REPRESENT THE **SON**.

SOURCE

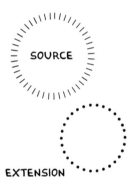

EXTENSION

GOD DIDN'T MAKE THIS UNIVERSE, WE DID. WE DREAMT IT UP BY TAKING LIBERTIES WITH OUR INHERITED POWER OF CREATION. WE TRIED TO MAKE SOMETHING SEEMINGLY **SEPARATE** FROM GOD.

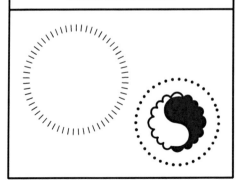

AND NOW WE ARE **AFRAID** TO WAKE UP BECAUSE, BY DREAMING, WE BECAME AFRAID OF GOD. IT IS REALLY AS **SIMPLE** AS THAT.

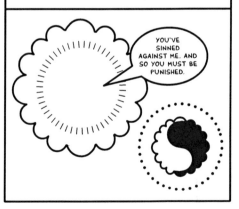

YOU'VE SINNED AGAINST ME. AND SO YOU MUST BE PUNISHED.

Y'SHUA'S STORY OF THE MAKING OF THIS UNIVERSE IS QUITE DIFFERENT FROM THE OLD **ADAM AND EVE** STORY. THE ADAM AND EVE CREATION STORY SUMS UP THE CONVOLUTED, **DUALISTIC** BELIEFS OF THE SLEEPING MIND, NOT THE **NONDUALISTIC** TRUTH OF THE AWAKENED MIND.

DUALISTIC MAKING

GOD MAKES A DUALISTIC WORLD AND MAKES A MAN NAMED ADAM WHO HE PLACES IN A PARADISE CALLED THE GARDEN OF EDEN.

THE SET-UP

ADAM IS ALLOWED TO DO WHATEVER HE WANTS EXCEPT HE CAN'T EAT FROM THE TREE OF KNOWLEDGE OF GOOD AND EVIL.

FOR ON THE DAY YOU EAT OF IT YOU SHALL SURELY DIE.

TREE OF JUDGMENT

MORE DUALISTIC MAKING

GOD MAKES A WOMAN NAMED EVE AS A COMPANION FOR ADAM.

THE FALL FOR THE SET-UP

EVE IS TEMPTED BY A SNAKE INTO EATING FROM THE TREE OF KNOWLEDGE, AND IN TURN EVE GETS ADAM TO EAT TOO.

SIN IS MADE REAL

ADAM AND EVE LOSE THEIR INNOCENCE AND HIDE. THEN GOD FINDS THEM AND BANISHES THEM FROM THE GARDEN OF EDEN.

SINCE JUDAISM WAS THE DOMINANT RELIGION IN Y'SHUA'S TIME, Y'SHUA'S TEACHINGS WERE MERELY TRANSFORMED INTO AN ELABORATED FORM OF JUDAISM.

THAT IS WHY THE CRUCIFIXION OF Y'SHUA IS SO DOMINANT IN CONVENTIONAL CHRISTIANITY.

IMAGE BASED ON THE YELLOW CHRIST BY PAUL GAUGUIN

JUST AS JUDAISM REPLACED THE OLD PRACTICE OF WORSHIPING MULTIPLE GODS WITH THE PRACTICE OF WORSHIPING A SINGLE GOD --

-- THE OLD JEWISH PRACTICE OF SACRIFICING THINGS LIKE GOATS TO GOD WAS REPLACED BY CHRISTIANITY WITH THE CRUCIFIXION OF Y'SHUA AS THE ULTIMATE SACRIFICE TO GOD.

WHAT Y'SHUA TAUGHT WAS ACTUALLY CLOSER TO BUDDHISM THAN WHAT WE OFTEN FIND IN CONVENTIONAL CHRISTIANITY.

HEAVEN IS WITHIN.

CONVENTIONAL CHRISTIANITY MOST OFTEN TRIES TO AVOID THE MIND; IT INSTEAD TENDS TO LOOK OUTWARD.

IT GETS PREOCCUPIED WITH CHANGING ILLUSIONS INSTEAD OF THE MIND THAT MADE THE ILLUSIONS.

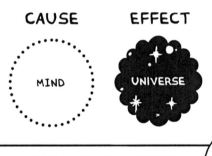

CAUSE

MIND

EFFECT

UNIVERSE

IT TRIES TO CHANGE EFFECTS INSTEAD OF THE CAUSE.

Y'SHUA AND BUDDHA BOTH EMPHASIZED THE PRIMACY OF MIND.

BUT UNLIKE BUDDHA, Y'SHUA ALSO EMPHASIZED GOD.

I AND THE FATHER ARE ONE.

BUDDHA WOKE UP, BUT Y'SHUA WENT ALL THE WAY BACK HOME TO GOD.

I AM AWAKE.

BY GOING ALL THE WAY BACK HOME TO GOD, Y'SHUA REMEMBERED THE TRUTH ABOUT GOD.

AND THE TRUTH ABOUT GOD IS MUCH DIFFERENT THAN THE CLASSIC PERSONIFIED UNIVERSE CREATING GOD OF CONVENTIONAL RELIGION.

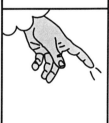

30

THAT GOD IS A LIE THAT ACTUALLY KEEPS PEOPLE DREAMING AND AFRAID TO WAKE UP.

THAT GOD IS A GOD OF DUALISM. THAT GOD IS TEMPERAMENTAL, CREATES IMPERFECT, CORRUPTIBLE THINGS, RECOGNIZES SEPARATION, PUNISHES, HAS A GENUINE ADVERSARY THAT SOME CALL THE DEVIL, AND PLAYS FAVORITES.

THAT GOD IS THE GOD OF DREAMING; IT IS A **FALSE** GOD.

THUS, IT COULD BE SAID THAT TO FIND THE REAL GOD REQUIRES BECOMING A **DUALISTIC GOD ATHEIST**; IT REQUIRES NOT BEING COMPLACENT IN PAYING HOMAGE TO SOMEONE WHO IS REALISTICALLY A CRUEL, DUALISTIC MORON.

PULL MY FINGER. I DARE YOU.

THERE ARE PLENTY OF REGULAR ATHEISTS IN THIS WORLD -- MANY OF WHICH ARE ACTUALLY MORE AGNOSTIC THAN TRULY ATHEISTIC -- BUT THERE AREN'T YET MANY DUALISTIC GOD ATHEISTS.

ATHEIST: DOESN'T BELIEVE IN THE EXISTENCE OF GOD(S).

AGNOSTIC: DOUBT OVER THE EXISTENCE OR NON-EXISTENCE OF GOD(S).

THEIST: BELIEVES IN THE EXISTENCE OF GOD(S).

A REGULAR ATHEIST IS IN GENERAL SOMEONE WHO THINKS DUALISTICALLY AND TAKES SMUG SOLACE IN THE LACK OF EMPIRICAL EVIDENCE SUPPORTING THE EXISTENCE OF THE DUALISTIC GOD OF MOST CONVENTIONAL RELIGIONS.

THERE IS NO **REASON** TO BELIEVE IN GOD.

CONVERSELY, A DUALISTIC GOD ATHEIST IS SOMEONE WHO THINKS NONDUALISTICALLY AND SO CANNOT ACCEPT A DUALISTIC GOD.

GOD CAN'T BE PERFECT LOVE AND ALSO A UNIVERSE-CREATING, UNIVERSE-MANIPULATING PSYCHO.

31

A **DUALISTIC GOD ATHEIST** SEES THE LACK OF EVIDENCE SUPPORTING THE EXISTENCE OF A DUALISTIC GOD AS EVIDENCE THAT GOD ISN'T DUALISTIC -- NOT THAT THERE IS NO GOD.

GOD DIDN'T CREATE THIS UNIVERSE. BUT THAT DOESN'T MEAN THERE IS NO GOD.

WHILE FEW PEOPLE IN THIS WORLD ARE REALLY DUALISTIC GOD ATHEISTS, MANY ARE AT LEAST **DUALISTIC GOD AGNOSTICS**; WHICH MEANS, THEY HAVE THEIR DOUBTS ABOUT DUALISTIC NOTIONS OF GOD.

SINCE RELIGIONS ARE MOSTLY JUST SOCIAL CLUBS, MANY PEOPLE SUPERFICIALLY PATRONIZE DUALISTIC NOTIONS OF GOD TO FIT IN SOCIALLY; BUT DEEP DOWN THEY ARE **DUALISTIC GOD AGNOSTICS**.

CHURCH OF THE SOCIALITES

THE THINKING OF DUALISTIC GOD AGNOSTICS IS ONLY **SEMIDUALISTIC** AND EXHIBITS SHREDS OF NONDUALISM.

I BELIEVE THAT GOD IS PERFECT LOVE -- BUT I DON'T KNOW HOW THAT FITS IN WITH THE REST OF THE STORY.

IN THE BIBLE, THE GOSPELS OF MARK AND MATTHEW TRIED TO MAKE Y'SHUA HIMSELF OUT TO BE A DUALISTIC GOD AGNOSTIC. WHILE DYING ON THE CROSS, THEY TRIED TO QUOTE Y'SHUA AS SAYING:

MY GOD, MY GOD, WHY HAVE YOU FORSAKEN ME?

THAT QUOTE IS OF COURSE **FALSE**, JUST LIKE MUCH OF THE STUFF ATTRIBUTED TO Y'SHUA IN THE BIBLE.

BUT THAT SHOULD COME AS NO SURPRISE SEEING AS THE **CANONICAL GOSPELS** OF THE BIBLE WERE WRITTEN MANY DECADES AFTER Y'SHUA'S DEATH BY PEOPLE WHO WEREN'T EVEN THERE WITH Y'SHUA AND WHO HAD THEIR OWN LIMITED AND DISTORTED SPIRITUAL UNDERSTANDING.

THE LIFE AND TIMES OF Y'SHUA WERE MANIPULATED TO FIT ANCIENT MYTHS AND PROPHECIES.

THE MOST ACCURATE GOSPEL IS THE **GOSPEL OF THOMAS**, WHO WAS ONE OF Y'SHUA'S TWELVE APOSTLES.

THE GOSPEL OF THOMAS WAS ORIGINALLY AN UNFINISHED RECORD OF SOME OF THE **SAYINGS** OF Y'SHUA.

HOWEVER, THE EARLY CHRISTIAN CHURCH HAD NO INTEREST IN THE TEACHINGS OF THAT GOSPEL. SO, IT WAS DESTROYED.

THAT IS BECAUSE THE EARLY CHRISTIAN CHURCH WAS FOUNDED ON THE THEOLOGY OF THE PHARISEE **PAUL**, NOT Y'SHUA.

PAUL, OR MORE ACCURATELY SAUL OF TARSUS, WAS NOT A STUDENT OF Y'SHUA. PAUL PERSECUTED EARLY FOLLOWERS OF Y'SHUA. HOWEVER, AROUND 33 A.D., PAUL JOINED THE CHRISTIAN CAUSE.

IF YOU CAN'T BEAT THEM, JOIN THEM.

IN JOINING THE CHRISTIAN CAUSE, PAUL BOTCHED Y'SHUA'S TEACHINGS TO FORM A KIND OF **JUDAISM 2.0**. PAUL'S JUDAISM 2.0 PROVED POPULAR. CONSEQUENTLY, THE THEOLOGY OF PAUL, NOT Y'SHUA, IS WHAT BECAME CHRISTIANITY.

THE ONLY REASON WE KNOW ABOUT THE DESTROYED GOSPEL OF THOMAS TODAY IS BECAUSE A MODIFIED COPY OF IT WAS DISCOVERED BURIED IN A SEALED JAR IN NAG HAMMADI, EGYPT IN 1945.

THE NAG HAMMADI COPY OF THE GOSPEL OF THOMAS CONTAINS SOME EXTRA SAYING THAT Y'SHUA DIDN'T ACTUALLY SAY AND THAT THOMAS DIDN'T ACTUALLY WRITE.

HOWEVER, THE NAG HAMMADI COPY OF THE GOSPEL OF THOMAS IS STILL THE MOST ACCURATE HISTORICAL RECORD OF WHAT Y'SHUA ACTUALLY SAID AND TAUGHT.

BUT ENOUGH ABOUT THAT SUBJECT. DWELLING UPON THE **DUBIOUS** AND **CONVOLUTED** HISTORY OF RELIGIONS IS JUST A MEANS OF STAYING ASLEEP.

IT IS RELIGULOUS.

THE FACT IS THAT THE FURTHER AWAY SOMETHING GETS FROM ITS ORIGINAL SOURCE, THE MORE DISTORTED IT BECOMES.

THIS IS NOT A PENCIL --

-- IT IS A REPRESENTATIVE DRAWING.

AND THAT SAME PRINCIPLE APPLIES TO THE ORIGINAL SOURCE KNOWN AS GOD.

THIS IS NOT GOD --

-- IT IS A SYMBOLIC DRAWING.

WHAT MADE Y'SHUA SO GREAT WAS THAT HE KNEW THE TRUE GOD.

HE TOTALLY AWAKENED AND RETURNED ALL THE WAY HOME TO GOD.

Y'SHUA KNEW THAT THE TRUE GOD IS PURE ONENESS...PURELY NONDUALISTIC... PERFECT LOVE.

PERFECT LOVE

THE GREAT TRUTH IS THAT **GOD IS** AND THAT NOTHING SEPARATE FROM GOD IS REAL.

AND THAT TRUTH IS THE FOUNDATION UPON WHICH WE CAN UNDERSTAND WHAT THIS DREAM UNIVERSE IS ALL ABOUT.

THIS UNIVERSE IS AN ATTEMPT AT MAKING SOMETHING SEPARATE FROM GOD.

BUT THE IDEA OF SOMETHING SEPARATE FROM GOD IS **ANTITHETIC** TO GOD BECAUSE GOD IS PURE ONENESS.

THUS, ANYTHING SEPARATE FROM GOD IS ULTIMATELY UNREAL AND AT MOST A TEMPORARY DREAM.

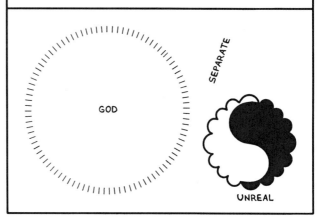

THAT IS WHAT THIS UNIVERSE IS; IT IS A **DREAM** OF **SEPARATION** FROM GOD; IT IS A DREAM OF BEING A SEPARATE, SPECIAL INDIVIDUAL, LIKE THE PRODIGAL SON.

BUT WORDS ARE MERELY SYMBOLS; THEY ARE THE THINGS OF DREAMS.

ONENESS WITH GOD IS A STATE OF PURE CREATION AND ENDLESS LOVE. IN ONENESS, THERE ARE NO OPPOSITES LIKE MALE AND FEMALE, DARKNESS AND LIGHT; ONENESS IS FORMLESS AND ETERNAL.

SO, FOR THE RECORD, GOD DOES NOT HAVE A PENIS, OR EVEN KNOW WHAT A PENIS IS.

GOD AS THE **FATHER** IS JUST A METAPHOR THAT IS PALATABLE TO PHALLOCENTRIC SOCIETIES.

UPON FIRST CONTEMPLATING THE IDEA OF ONENESS, PEOPLE OFTEN TRY TO DISMISS IT AS SEEMINGLY BORING.

THAT SEEMS REALLY BORING -- THERE'S NO CONFLICT.

BUT THAT IS MERELY A MISINFORMED DEFENSE AGAINST WAKING UP, BECAUSE THEY THINK OF ONENESS AS AN ISOLATED FRAGMENT INSTEAD OF TOTAL WHOLENESS. SUCH THINKING IS AN ARTIFACT OF THE BELIEF IN DUALISM.

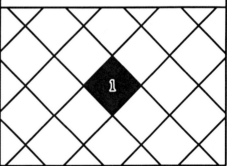

THE IDEA OF ONE IN THIS UNIVERSE IS ALWAYS A FRACTION AND NEVER A WHOLE. THAT IS WHY MOST PEOPLE THINK THAT 1+1=2. IN REALITY, 1+1=1. ONLY A **FRACTION** OF ONE, LIKE 1/2, MAKES 2.

ALL **THINGS** IN THIS DREAM ARE SYMBOLS OF FRACTIONS. THEY ARE ALL FRACTIONS OF FRACTIONS.

AND THAT INCLUDES NUMBERS. NUMBERS ARE THE IDEA OF ONE SPLIT APART INTO COUNTLESS ONES.

$1 = \frac{1}{76}$

FRACTIONS REPRESENT THE REALM BETWEEN ZERO AND ONE, OR, IN OTHER WORDS, BETWEEN OBLIVION AND WHOLENESS.

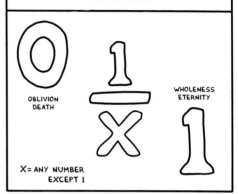

OBLIVION
DEATH

WHOLENESS
ETERNITY

X = ANY NUMBER
EXCEPT 1

AND INCIDENTALLY, THAT IS WHY I MADE THE CHAPTERS OF THIS BOOK FRACTIONS.

$X = 9$

I WOULD HAVE MADE THE PAGE NUMBERS FRACTIONS TOO, BUT I DIDN'T WANT TO CONFUSE PEOPLE TOO MUCH.

YOU MAY HAVE HEARD PEOPLE SAY THAT ONE IS THE LONELIEST NUMBER. BUT THAT IS INCORRECT.

ONE AS A FRAGMENT IS THE LONELIEST NUMBER, BECAUSE IT IS THE IDEA OF SEPARATION FROM ONE AS A WHOLE -- ONENESS.

THERE IS NO LONELINESS IN TRUE ONENESS BECAUSE IN TRUE ONENESS THERE IS NOTHING LACKING.

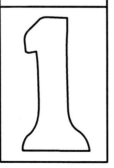

THERE IS NO SYMBOLIC DESCRIPTION OF ONENESS THAT CAN SATISFY THE INTELLECT, BECAUSE ONENESS IS A STATE OF MIND THAT IS ANTITHETICAL TO DUALISM. AND DUALISM IS NECESSARY FOR INTELLECTUAL FORMULATION.

IN THAT SENSE, ONENESS IS THE ONLY THING THAT CAN BE TRULY **KNOWN** -- EVERYTHING ELSE IS ILLUSORY KNOWLEDGE.

THERE ARE THINGS IN THIS DREAM REMINISCENT OF THE STATE OF ONENESS WITH GOD, LIKE LOVING RELATIONSHIPS AND BEAUTY --

-- BUT THOSE ARE EXTREMELY FEEBLE COMPARISONS AT BEST. THEY ARE JUST FRAIL SYMBOLS THAT ATTEMPT TO SUBSTITUTE THE TRUTH.

GOD IS ONENESS AND ONENESS IS BEYOND ALL SYMBOLS -- BEYOND ALL FRACTIONS. THAT IS WHY YOU SHOULDN'T TRY TO MAKE **IMAGES** OF GOD; YOU'LL END UP MAKING GOD OUT TO BE A FRACTION INSTEAD OF PERFECT WHOLENESS; YOU'LL END UP MAKING GOD OUT TO BE AN ILLUSION.

THE PERSONIFIED GOD

GOD AS A POWERFUL SUPERMAN.

THE PANTHEISTIC GOD

GOD AS THE BEAUTY OF NATURE.

THE GOD SUBSTITUTE

GOD AS SOMETHING FOUND IN THE WORLD.

THE SYMBOL IS NOT THE EXPERIENCE.

YET, SYMBOLS CAN POINT THE WAY OUT OF THIS DREAM AND TO THE EXPERIENCE.

IF THERE WASN'T A WAY OUT OF THIS DREAM, THIS DREAM WOULD BE REAL.

FORTUNATELY, THAT IS AS IMPOSSIBLE AS THIS DREAM ITSELF.

CHAPTER THREE NINTHS

HOW THE IMPOSSIBLE NEVER REALLY HAPPENED

ALTHOUGH THE HISTORY OF THIS DREAM UNIVERSE CAN BE SUMMED UP IN A LITTLE STORY LIKE THE PRODIGAL SON --

-- OR EVEN A MATHEMATICAL EQUATION --

(HINT: SOLVE IT)

$$1-1\frac{(1-1)}{X}=1$$

-- TO REALLY UNDERSTAND THE HISTORY OF THIS DREAM, WE NEED TO LOOK AT IT IN DETAIL **STEP** BY **STEP**. SO, LET'S DO THAT.

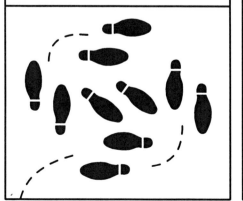

BEFORE THE BEGINNING, THERE WAS AND STILL IS THE ONENESS OF GOD, WHICH WE'LL CALL **ONE-MINDEDNESS**.

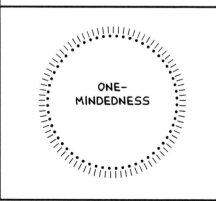

ONE-MINDEDNESS

CONCEPTS LIKE BEGINNINGS AND ENDINGS ARE IMPOSSIBLE IN ONENESS.

SO, NATURALLY, MOST PEOPLE ARE INCLINED TO ASK, HOW DID THE IMPOSSIBLE HAPPEN THEN?

WELL, THE SHORT ANSWER IS THAT IT DIDN'T.

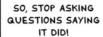

SO, STOP ASKING QUESTIONS SAYING IT DID!

IF THE HEAVENLY LOVE OF ONENESS WAS COMPLETELY SATISFYING, WHY WOULD WE CHOOSE TO DREAM THAT WE LEFT?

IF GOD IS PERFECT AND UNIFIED, HOW COULD AN IMPERFECT THOUGHT HAVE POSSIBLY ARISEN WITHIN SUCH A MIND?

EVEN IF WE WAKE UP, HOW DO WE KNOW WE WON'T FALL ASLEEP AGAIN?

DREAMS ARE NOT REAL, SO THEY DO NOT REALLY HAPPEN -- DESPITE THE DELUSIONS OF THOSE LOST IN DREAMS.

GOD KNOWS NOTHING OF THIS DREAM BECAUSE FORTUNATELY GOD ISN'T INSANE. IN GOD'S REALITY, THIS DREAM WAS OVER AS SOON AS IT BEGAN.

BUT THIS DREAM CONTAINS SOMETHING REALITY DOESN'T CONTAIN, WHICH MAKES IT SEEM FOR US TO CARRY ON. THAT SOMETHING IS **TIME**.

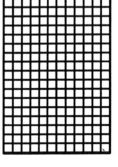

TIME IS A SEPARATION IDEA BORN OF SEEMINGLY SPLITTING UP ETERNITY.

BEGINNINGS AND ENDINGS ARISE FROM THE CONCEPT OF TIME. TIME IS INTERTWINED WITH SPACE TO FORM WHAT **EINSTEIN** CALLED SPACETIME.

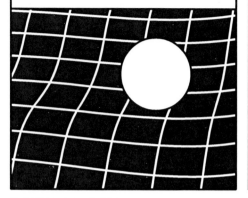

AND ANY PHYSICIST WORTH HIS OR HER SALT WHO HAS LOOKED CLOSELY AT THIS UNIVERSE CAN ATTEST TO THE VARIABILITY OF SPACETIME.

TIME CEASES AT THE SPEED OF LIGHT. AS AN OBJECT APPROACHES THE SPEED OF LIGHT, IT APPROACHES INFINITE MASS. A PERSON IN A SPACESHIP TRAVELING NEAR THE SPEED OF LIGHT, OR PERCHED ON THE EVENT HORIZON OF A SUPER MASSIVE BLACK HOLE, COULD TRAVEL HUNDREDS, THOUSAND, EVEN MILLIONS OF YEARS INTO THE FUTURE (RELATIVE TO TIME ON EARTH) WITHIN A FEW MINUTES.

SPACETIME IS A SEPARATION IDEA; IT IS NATURALLY UNREAL.

IN REALITY, THERE IS NO SPACETIME BETWEEN YOU AND GOD. NOR IS THERE SPACETIME BETWEEN YOU AND ME. I AM YOU AND YOU ARE ME AND WE ARE IN REALITY ONE WITH GOD.

YOU CAN'T DO THAT

IN ONENESS

WE ARE ESSENTIALLY THE SON OF GOD, ALSO KNOWN AS CHRIST, WHICH MAKES GOD OUR AUTHOR, OUR SOURCE.

WE ARE AN ENDLESSLY CREATIVE **EXTENSION** OF GOD. THERE IS NO DEMARCATION BETWEEN WHERE WE BEGIN AND GOD ENDS. WE ARE ONE MIND.

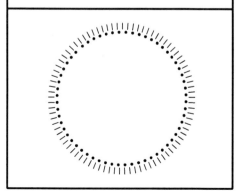

NOTHING THAT GOD KNOWS NOT EXISTS. AND WHAT GOD KNOWS EXISTS FOREVER, CHANGELESSLY. [1]

LET THAT STATEMENT SINK IN FOR A MOMENT.

JUST AS THE THOUGHTS WE THINK ARE IN OUR MIND, WE ARE IN THE MIND THAT THOUGHT OF US: GOD. THEREFORE, WHAT EXISTS WITHIN GOD'S MIND IS FOREVER ONE, ETERNALLY UNITED AND AT PEACE. [2]

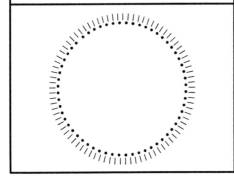

BUT RIGHT NOW, WE ARE HAVING A DREAM OF SOMETHING DIFFERENT: **MULTIPLE MINDEDNESS**.

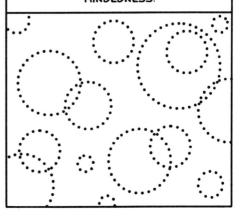

THIS DREAM IS A MISPERCEPTION AND A MISCREATION. CREATION IS ONENESS WITH GOD AND THUS ALWAYS INCLUDES GOD.

BUT THIS DREAM IS AN INSANE ATTEMPT AT INVERSE CREATION, WHEREBY WE'VE TRIED TO CREATE SOMETHING SEPARATE FROM GOD.

IT ALL STARTED WITH A TINY, MAD IDEA. [3]

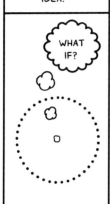

THAT TINY, MAD IDEA WAS MADE INNOCENTLY, BUT IT WAS NONETHELESS A MAD IDEA; IT WAS SO MAD THAT WE STILL HAVEN'T GOTTEN OVER IT; WE CONTINUE TO REPEAT THAT MAD IDEA EVERY MICROSECOND OF EVERYDAY. THAT MAD IDEA IS WHAT KEEPS THIS DREAM SEEMINGLY GOING.

THAT MAD IDEA WAS THE IDEA OF HAVING A THOUGHT UNSHARED BY GOD -- IT WAS A THOUGHT OF BEING SEPARATE FROM GOD AND THUS OF BEING **SPECIAL**.

WHAT IF I HAD MORE THAN EVERYTHING? WHAT IF I HAD A PRIVATE THOUGHT -- SEPARATE FROM GOD? WHAT IF I WAS SPECIAL?

FROM THE VIEWPOINT OF ONENESS, THAT IS IMPOSSIBLE.

SUCH A THOUGHT IS THE APEX OF ABSURDITY --

PRIVATE THOUGHT

ABSURDITY

-- IT IS ESSENTIALLY THE GREATEST JOKE EVER TOLD; IT IS THE JOKE FROM WHICH ALL THE HUMOR IN THIS DREAM UNIVERSE WAS EVER DERIVED.

THE HUMOR CODE
(THE SECRET TO MAKING PEOPLE LAUGH)

YES + NO = FUNNY
NO + NO = SERIOUS
YES + YES = SERIOUS

TO MAKE PEOPLE LAUGH, ALL YOU HAVE TO DO IS MAKE THEM SAY YES AND NO SIMULTANEOUSLY IN THEIR MINDS. A SIMULTANEOUS YES AND NO CAUSES AN INNER TENSION THAT IS RELEASED THROUGH LAUGHTER.

HOWEVER, ALTHOUGH THAT THOUGHT WAS A JOKE, THAT THOUGHT GAVE RISE TO DUALITY AND THUS CONSCIOUSNESS.

IT GAVE RISE TO THE IDEA OF US VERSUS GOD AS TWO SEPARATE MINDS.

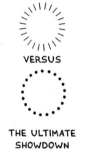

VERSUS

THE ULTIMATE SHOWDOWN

IT MADE **ONE-MINDEDNESS** JUST A **MEMORY**. AND WITH ONE-MINDEDNESS JUST A MEMORY, OUR MIND BECAME SPLIT INTO A **RIGHT MIND** AND A **WRONG MIND**.

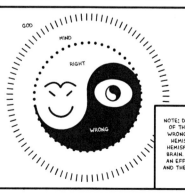

GOD
MIND
RIGHT
WRONG

NOTE: DON'T CONFUSE THE IDEA OF THE RIGHT MIND AND THE WRONG MIND WITH THE RIGHT HEMISPHERE AND THE LEFT HEMISPHERE OF THE PHYSICAL BRAIN. THE PHYSICAL BRAIN IS AN EFFECT OF THE SPLIT MIND AND THEREFORE IS BY NO MEANS ITS CAUSE.

OUR RIGHT MIND RETAINED THE MEMORY OF GOD AS REALITY WHILE OUR WRONG MIND ENTERTAINED THE IDEA OF SEPARATION AS REALITY.

1
0

RIGHT MIND	VERSUS	WRONG MIND

BORROWING FROM CHRISTIAN TERMINOLOGY, WE'LL CALL OUR RIGHT MIND **THE HOLY SPIRIT**. THE HOLY SPIRIT IS THE VOICE FOR ONENESS. THE HOLY SPIRIT COULD ALSO BE CALLED OUR HIGHER OR TRUE SELF; IT IS THE SELF WITH WHICH Y'SHUA IDENTIFIED.

BORROWING FROM PSYCHOLOGICAL TERMINOLOGY, WE'LL CALL OUR WRONG MIND **THE EGO**. THE EGO IS THE VOICE FOR SEPARATION, DIVISION, CONFLICT, AND INDIVIDUALITY. THE EGO IS WHAT WE USUALLY REFER TO WHEN WE USE THE WORD **I**.

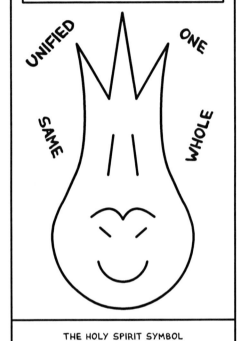

UNIFIED   ONE
SAME   WHOLE

THE HOLY SPIRIT SYMBOL

INDIVIDUAL   SEPARATE
UNIQUE   SPECIAL

THE EGO SYMBOL

WITH THE SPLIT OF OUR MIND CAME A CONSCIOUS CHOICE:

SIDE WITH THE HOLY SPIRIT AND LAUGH AWAY THE ABSURD IDEA OF SEPARATION, OR SIDE WITH THE EGO AND TAKE THE IDEA SERIOUSLY?

44

THE HOLY SPIRIT'S INTERPRETATION OF THE IDEA OF SEPARATION WAS, AND STILL IS, TO **LAUGH IT AWAY** BY RECOGNIZING ITS ABSURD UNREALITY RELATIVE TO THE TRUTH.

HOWEVER, THE EGO'S INTERPRETATION OF THE IDEA OF SEPARATION WAS, AND STILL IS, TO TAKE IT SERIOUSLY.

SO, OBVIOUSLY, WE FOOLISHLY CHOSE TO TAKE THE JOKE SERIOUSLY AND THUS SIDED WITH THE WRONG-MINDED EGO. THAT IS WHY WE ARE SEEMINGLY HERE TODAY.

THE HUMOR CODE

YES + NO = FUNNY
NO + NO = SERIOUS
YES + YES = SERIOUS

ILLUSION = YES

ILLUSION + NO = FUNNY
ILLUSION + YES = SERIOUS

AND THE REASON WE ENDED UP TAKING THE JOKE SERIOUSLY WAS BECAUSE THE EGO CAME UP WITH AN IDEA WE FOUND TEMPTING.

WE LIKED THE SELF-AUTHORSHIP IDEA AND THEREFORE CHOSE TO FOLLOW THE WRONG-MINDED LEAD OF THE EGO.

BY CHOOSING TO FOLLOW THE LEAD OF THE EGO, WE REPRESSED OUR RIGHT MIND: THE HOLY SPIRIT.

CONSEQUENTLY, WE LOST OUR SANITY AND THINGS STARTED GETTING SCARY.

BY CHOOSING THE EGO, WE CHOSE A SELF-INVENTED, HATEFUL THING BUILT OF GUILT.

SO, NEEDLESS TO SAY, BY CHOOSING THE EGO, WE STARTED GETTING ALL KINDS OF CRAZY IDEAS. THAT IS BECAUSE WE WERE NOW ENTERTAINING THE IDEA OF DUALITY WITH FULL FORCE. EVERYTHING WE HAD KNOWN IN OUR ONENESS WITH GOD SUDDENLY BECAME COUNTERBALANCED BY AN OPPOSITE IDEA.

ABSENCE PRESENCE ACCEPT REFUSE ACCURATE INACCURATE ADVANTAGE DISADVANTAGE ALIVE DEAD ALWAYS NEVER ANCIENT MODERN ANSWER QUESTION, QUERY APPROVAL DISAPPROVAL APPROACHED RECEDED, DEPARTED ABUNDANT SCARCE ADMIT DENY ADVANCE RETREAT, RETIRE ARTIFICIAL NATURAL ARRIVAL DEPARTURE ASCEND DESCEND ATTACK DEFENSE ATTRACTIVE REPULSIVE ATTENTION INATTENTION ASLEEP AWAKE ALLY ENEMY AGREE DISAGREE BAD GOOD BACKWARD FORWARD, ONWARD BEND STRAIGHTEN BEAUTIFUL UGLY BEGINNING ENDING BELOW ABOVE BENT STRAIGHT BIG SMALL, LITTLE BLUNT SHARP BETTER WORSE BEST WORST BLAME PRAISE BLESS CURSE BITTER SWEET BORROW LEND BRAVERY COWARDICE BUILD DESTROY, DEMOLISH BOLD TIMID, MEEK BRIGHT DULL BROAD NARROW CLEAR VAGUE, CLOUDY CAREFUL RUSH, CARELESS CALM TROUBLED CAPABLE INCAPABLE CAPTIVITY FREEDOM, LIBERTY CELLAR ATTIC CHEAP DEAR, EXPENSIVE CLOSE DISTANT CLEVER STUPID COLD HOT COMBINE SEPARATE CLOCKWISE ANTI-CLOCKWISE CORRECT INCORRECT CONCEAL REVEAL COME GO COMMON RARE COMFORT DISCOMFORT COURAGE COWARDICE CRUEL KIND COURTEOUS DISCOURTEOUS, RUDE CUNNING SIMPLE DAINTY CLUMSY DANGER SAFETY DARK LIGHT DEEP SHALLOW DECREASE INCREASE DEFINITE INDEFINITE DEMAND SUPPLY DESPAIR HOPE DISAPPEAR APPEAR DISEASE HEALTH DISCOURAGE ENCOURAGE DISMAL CHEERFUL DOCTOR PATIENT DRY WET DULL CLEAR, BRIGHT DUSK DAWN EARLY LATE EASY DIFFICULT EBB FLOW EAST WEST ECONOMIZE WASTE ENCOURAGE DISCOURAGE ENTRANCE EXIT EMPLOYER EMPLOYEE EMPTY FULL EXCITED CALM END BEGINNING EXPAND CONTRACT EXPENSIVE INEXPENSIVE, CHEAP EXPORT IMPORT EXTERIOR INTERIOR EXTERNAL INTERNAL FAIL SUCCEED FALSE TRUE FEEBLE STURDY STRONG, POWERFUL FOOLISH WISE FAST SLOW FEW MANY FAMOUS UNKNOWN FORELEGS HIND LEGS FAT THIN FIND LOSE FIRST LAST FREEDOM CAPTIVITY FOLD UNFOLD FREQUENT SELDOM FORGET REMEMBER FOUND LOST FRESH STALE FRIEND ENEMY FORTUNATE UNFORTUNATE FRANK SECRETIVE FULL EMPTY GENEROUS MEAN GENTLE ROUGH GATHER DISTRIBUTE GLAD SORRY GLOOMY CHEERFUL GIANT DWARF, PYGMY GRANTED REFUSED GREAT MINUTE, SMALL, LITTLE GUARDIAN WARD GUEST HOST GUILTY INNOCENT HAPPY SAD, MISERABLE HARD SOFT HARMFUL HARMLESS HASTEN DAWDLE HATE LOVE HEALTHY UNHEALTHY, ILL, DISEASED HERE THERE HEAVY LIGHT HEIGHT DEPTH HERO COWARD HILL VALLEY HORIZONTAL VERTICAL HINDER AID, HELP HONEST DISHONEST HUMBLE PROUD HUNGER THIRST IMITATION GENUINE IMMENSE TINY, MINUTE IMPRISON FREE INCLUDE EXCLUDE INCREASE DECREASE INHABITED UNINHABITED INFERIOR SUPERIOR INSIDE OUTSIDE INTELLIGENT UNINTELLIGENT, STUPID INHALE EXHALE INTERIOR EXTERIOR, OUTSIDE INTERESTING UNINTERESTING, DULL INTERNAL EXTERNAL INTENTIONAL ACCIDENTAL JOIN SEPARATE JUNIOR SENIOR JUSTICE INJUSTICE KING SUBJECT KNOWLEDGE IGNORANCE LAUGH CRY LAWFUL UNLAWFUL LAZY INDUSTRIOUS, ENERGETIC LAND SEA LANDLORD TENANT LARGE LITTLE SMALL LAST FIRST LAWYER CLIENT LECTURER STUDENT LENDER BORROWER LENGTHEN SHORTEN LEFT RIGHT LESS MORE LIGHT DARK, HEAVY LIKE DISLIKE, UNLIKE LIKELY UNLIKELY LEADER FOLLOWER LITTLE LARGE, MUCH, BIG LOFTY LOWLY LONG SHORT LOUD SOFT LOSS FIND, WIN LOW HIGH LOYAL DISLOYAL MAD SANE MAGNETIZE DEMAGNETIZE MALE FEMALE MASTER SERVANT MATURE IMMATURE MAXIMUM MINIMUM ME YOU MERRY MIRTHLESS, SAD MINORITY MAJORITY MISER SPENDTHRIFT MISUNDERSTAND UNDERSTAND NARROW WIDE NEAR FAR, DISTANT NEAT UNTIDY NEW OLD NIGHT DAY NOISY QUIET NORTH SOUTH OBEDIENT DISOBEDIENT ODD EVEN OFFER REFUSE OPEN SHUT OPTIMIST PESSIMIST OUT IN PARENT CHILD PAST PRESENT PATIENT IMPATIENT PEACE WAR PERMANENT TEMPORARY PLEASE DISPLEASE PLENTIFUL SCARCE POETRY PROSE POSSIBLE IMPOSSIBLE POVERTY WEALTH POWERFUL FEEBLE, WEAK POLITE IMPOLITE, RUDE PRIVATE PUBLIC PRUDENT IMPRUDENT PRETTY UNSIGHTLY, UGLY PURE IMPURE QUALIFIED UNQUALIFIED RAPID SLOW REGULARLY IRREGULARLY RICH POOR RIGHT WRONG, LEFT RIGID PLIABLE, SOFT ROUGH SMOOTH SATISFACTORY UNSATISFACTORY SECURITY INSECURITY SCATTER COLLECT SERIOUS TRIVIAL SECOND-HAND NEW SENSE NONSENSE SHOPKEEPER CUSTOMER SINGULAR PLURAL SIMPLE COMPLICATED SLIM THICK STOUT SOLID LIQUID SOBER DRUNK SPEAKER LISTENER SOUR SWEET SORROW JOY SOW REAP STAND LIE STRAIGHT CROOKED STRONG WEAK SUCCESS FAILURE SUNNY CLOUDY TAKE GIVE TALL SHORT TAME WILD TEACHER PUPIL THICK THIN TIGHT SLACK, LOOSE TOP BOTTOM TRANSPARENT OPAQUE TRUTH UNTRUTH, LIE UP DOWN VACANT OCCUPIED VALUABLE VALUELESS VICTORY DEFEAT VIRTUE VICE VISIBLE INVISIBLE VOLUNTARY COMPULSORY VOWEL CONSONANT WAX WANE WISDOM FOLLY WITHIN WITHOUT

WE STARTED BELIEVING THAT WE DESTROYED HEAVEN AND KILLED GOD. THE EGO INTERPRETED THAT IDEA FOR US AS SIN. WITH THE BELIEF IN SIN CAME THE CONCEPT OF PUNISHMENT AND THUS FEAR -- IT MADE GOD SEEM LIKE OUR ENEMY.

HERE RESTS GOD

THE KILLER ZOMBIE THAT WILL RISE FROM THE GRAVE AND SEEK A VENGEANCE WORSE THAN DEATH UPON US

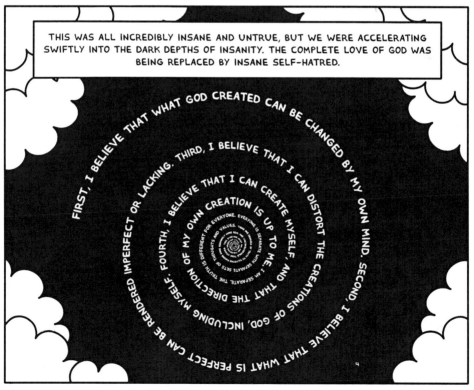

THIS WAS ALL INCREDIBLY INSANE AND UNTRUE, BUT WE WERE ACCELERATING SWIFTLY INTO THE DARK DEPTHS OF INSANITY. THE COMPLETE LOVE OF GOD WAS BEING REPLACED BY INSANE SELF-HATRED.

FIRST, I BELIEVE THAT WHAT GOD CREATED CAN BE CHANGED BY MY OWN MIND. SECOND, I BELIEVE THAT WHAT IS PERFECT CAN BE RENDERED IMPERFECT OR LACKING. THIRD, I BELIEVE THAT I CAN CREATE MYSELF, AND THAT THE DIRECTION OF MY OWN CREATION IS UP TO ME. FOURTH, I BELIEVE THAT I CAN DISTORT THE CREATIONS OF GOD, INCLUDING MYSELF.

WE WERE STARTING TO FEEL EXTREMELY BAD, WITH A CRUSHING, PAINFUL, AND TERRIFYING SENSE OF GUILT.

GUILT IS ESSENTIALLY SELF-HATE AND LEADS TO SELF-SABOTAGE.

THE PAST TENSE OF GUILT IS SIN AND THE FUTURE TENSE OF GUILT IS FEAR.

FROM SIN, GUILT, AND FEAR WE GET **TIME**. TIME IS THE ALTERNATIVE TO ETERNITY.

SIN
PAST

SIN IS THE BELIEF WE ACTUALLY SEPARATED FROM GOD -- THAT WE ATTACKED GOD AND BECAME OUR OWN AUTHOR.

GUILT
PRESENT

GUILT IS THE PRESENT EXPERIENCE OF BELIEVING WE SINNED.

FEAR
FUTURE

AND FEAR IS THE BELIEF THAT GOD WILL PUNISH US FOR OUR SIN -- BY DOING TO US WHAT WE BELIEVE WE DID TO GOD.

FORTUNATELY, THERE IS ONE MORE ASPECT TO TIME THAT HELPS US **COLLAPSE** TIME CALLED THE HOLY INSTANT. BUT MORE ON THAT LATER.

GUILTLESS
PRESENT

HOLY INSTANT

SINCE OUR NEWFOUND GUILT WAS PAINFUL, THE EGO GAVE US A **SOLUTION** TO SEEMINGLY GET RID OF IT. THE EGO SAID IT COULD GIVE US A **HIDING** PLACE WHERE WE COULD HAVE INDIVIDUALITY AND BE SAFE FROM **KILLER ZOMBIE GOD**; IT SAID WE COULD MAKE A SUBSTITUTE HEAVEN AND GET GOD OUT OF OUR MIND.

I HAVE A SOLUTION.

AND WITH THAT CAME THE BIG BANG, OR MORE ACCURATELY, THE BIG **PROJECTION**.

THE EGO TOOK OUR CRAZY, GUILT-LADEN EGO BELIEF SYSTEM ABOUT OUR SEEMING SEPARATION FROM GOD AND **DENIED** IT, WHICH MADE IT UNCONSCIOUS.

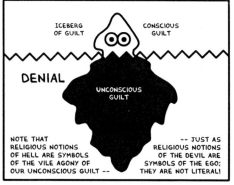

A PSYCHOLOGICAL RULE OF THE MIND ELUCIDATED BY **SIGMUND FREUD** IS THAT **DENIAL LEADS TO PROJECTION**. THEREFORE, AFTER WE DENIED THE GUILT IN OUR MIND, WE PROJECTED IT OUTWARD. WE LITERALLY WENT **OUT OF OUR MIND**.

OUR DENIED GUILT BECAME THE FILM (OR RECORDED MEDIA) FOR OUR BIG PROJECTION.

THE PROJECTION BECAME THE WITNESS TO THE STATE OF MIND THAT MADE THE PROJECTION; IT BECAME THE OUTSIDE PICTURE OF OUR INWARD CONDITION. ⁴

IN THEATHERS NOW

UNIVERSE OF THE LIVING DEAD*

THE PROJECTION SHATTERED OUR ONE MIND INTO COUNTLESS FRAGMENTS, ALL WITH THE ABILITY TO BLAME EACH OTHER FOR THE SEEMING SEPARATION FROM GOD.

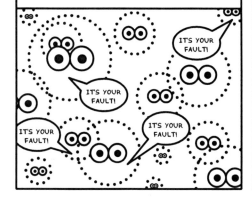

THOSE FRAGMENTS OF OUR ONE MIND ARE WHAT WE CALL **SOULS**. A SOUL IS AN INDIVIDUALIZED FRAGMENT OF OUR ONE DREAMING MIND.

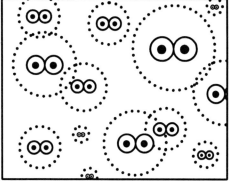

EACH FRAGMENT OF OUR ONE MIND CONTAINS THE WHOLE MIND BECAUSE THE STRUCTURE OF THE FRACTURE FROM ONENESS WAS FRACTAL.

A FRACTAL IS A FRAGMENT OF A WHOLE THAT CONTAINS THE WHOLE.

THAT MEANS THAT ALTHOUGH EACH MIND CONTAINS THE EGO'S CRAZY, GUILT-LADEN, SELF-SABOTAGING THOUGHT SYSTEM, EACH MIND ALSO CONTAINS THE HOLY SPIRIT'S CORRECTIVE THOUGHT SYSTEM.

PLUS, EACH MIND CONTAINS THE DECISION-MAKING ABILITY TO CHOOSE BETWEEN THE TWO THOUGHT SYSTEMS.

SOME SIMPLE EXAMPLES OF FRACTALS ARE A SQUARE MADE OF SQUARES --

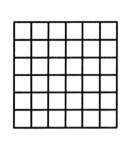

-- A TRIANGLE MADE OF TRIANGLES --

-- A TREE MADE OF TREES.

HOWEVER, THE **FUNDAMENTAL FRACTAL** OF THIS UNIVERSE IS NOT A FORM, OR SHAPE. FORM IS MERELY AN EFFECT OF THE FUNDAMENTAL FRACTAL WHEN IT IS PROJECTED.

FORM IS LIKE A HOLOGRAM. THUS, THE SEEMINGLY PHYSICAL WORLD WE SEE IS LIKE A HOLOGRAM. BUT THERE IS NO HOLOGRAM WITHOUT THE FUNDAMENTAL FRACTAL.

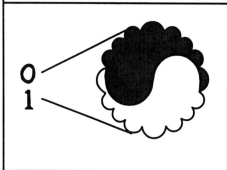

THE FUNDAMENTAL FRACTAL OF THIS UNIVERSE IS A **THOUGHT**: THE THOUGHT OF SEPARATION FROM ONENESS: THE IDEA OF HAVING A THOUGHT UNSHARED BY GOD.

OR, IN OTHER WORDS, THE FUNDAMENTAL FRACTAL OF THIS UNIVERSE IS **DUALITY**. DUALITY AMOUNTS TO A BINARY BIT OF INFORMATION.

IN BINARY CODE, SUCH AS COMPUTERS USE, A ONE REPRESENTS AN ON SWITCH WHILE A ZERO REPRESENTS AN OFF SWITCH. ON A UNIVERSAL SCALE, THE ENERGY FLOWING THROUGH AN ON SWITCH (1) IS THE INFINITE LIGHT OF HEAVENLY ONENESS (TRUE LOVE). CONVERSELY, AN OFF SWITCH (0) STOPS THE INFINITE FLOW OF ENERGY. THE NET RESULT OF THE INTERACTION OF TURNING THE INFINITE LIGHT OF ONENESS ON AND OFF IS THIS DREAM UNIVERSE: THE UNIVERSE OF THE LIVING (1) DEAD (0).

IN MATHEMATICAL TERMS, THE HOLY SPIRIT REPRESENTS ONE AS A WHOLE, WHILE THE EGO REPRESENTS ZERO, OR THE COMPLETE ANNIHILATION OF ONENESS.

 BINARY CODE

A CODE OF ONE EQUALS HEAVEN.
1

A CODE OF ZERO EQUALS OBLIVION.
0

AND A MIXED CODE OF MULTIPLE ONES AND ZEROS EQUALS THIS DREAM UNIVERSE.
01000010011010010110111001100001 01110010

FORTUNATELY, ZERO IS IMPOSSIBLE; ONLY ONENESS IS TRUE. THEREFORE, THE REALM OF THE EGO RESTS BETWEEN ONE AND ZERO, IN AN ILLUSORY, FRACTIONAL REALM SUSTAINED BY THE FRACTAL OF DUALISM.

ON EVERY LEVEL OF THIS PROJECTED UNIVERSE, FROM THE LEVEL OF GALAXIES, TO THE LEVEL OF RELATIONSHIPS, TO THE LEVEL OF SUBATOMIC PARTICLES, WE **REPEAT** THE FRACTAL OF DUALISM.

THUS, OUR INDIVIDUAL MINDS, PSYCHOLOGIES, AND EXPERIENCES IN THIS DREAM ARE PART OF A LARGER, INTEGRATED, MODULAR HIERARCHY WITH THE SAME ARCHITECTURE AS OUR INDIVIDUAL MINDS, PSYCHOLOGIES, AND EXPERIENCES.

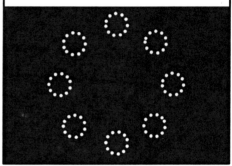

ON THE PROJECTED PHYSICAL LEVEL, REPEATING THE FRACTAL OF DUALISM IS A PROCESS OF **BONDING** AND **SPLITTING**.

THAT BONDING AND SPLITTING PROCESS IS WHAT SEEMINGLY MAKES BODIES.

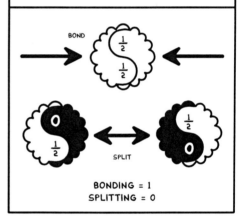

AND BODIES WERE THE **FINAL INGREDIENT** IN THE **MISCREATION** OF THIS UNIVERSE.

THE WAY A MIND FRAGMENT, OR SOUL, EXPERIENCES THIS DREAM IS THROUGH A BODY.

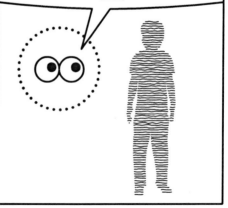

BODIES ARE PROJECTED PUPPETS OF THE MIND THAT PROVIDE MIND FRAGMENTS WITH DIFFERENT AND LIMITED POINTS OF VIEW FROM WHICH TO EXPERIENCE THIS DREAM.

YET, DESPITE OUR INDIVIDUAL POINTS OF VIEW, THERE IS STILL ONLY ONE DREAM AND ONE MIND DOING THE DREAMING.

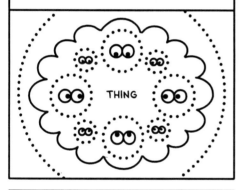

THAT IS WHY WE ALL HAVE COMMON EXPERIENCES OF **THINGS** IN THIS DREAM UPON WHICH WE CAN AGREE. THAT AGREEMENT IS WHAT MAKES SCIENTIFIC KNOWLEDGE POSSIBLE.

THING

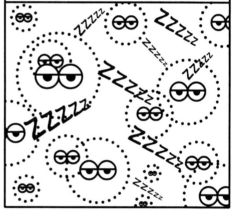

EACH MIND FRAGMENT, OR SOUL, DREAMS UNTIL IT WAKES UP.

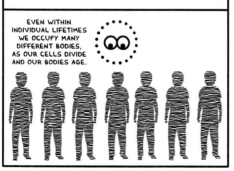

CONSEQUENTLY, EACH MIND FRAGMENT SEEMINGLY OCCUPIES MANY DIFFERENT BODIES IN THE COURSE OF ITS DREAMING. WHICH IS TO SAY, MINDS REINCARNATE -- OR, MORE ACCURATELY, MINDS DREAM FROM THE VIEWPOINT OF DIFFERENT CHARACTERS.

EVEN WITHIN INDIVIDUAL LIFETIMES WE OCCUPY MANY DIFFERENT BODIES, AS OUR CELLS DIVIDE AND OUR BODIES AGE.

SO-CALLED INCARNATION IS ACTUALLY THE RESULT OF TRYING TO DENY GUILT. THE GUILTLESS DON'T INCARNATE.

SO, CONTRARY TO COMMON MISPERCEPTION, CHILDREN AREN'T BORN INTO THIS WORLD AS INNOCENT, CLEAN SLATES THAT ARE THEN CORRUPTED BY THE WORLD; THEY COME WITH THE EGO THOUGHT SYSTEM INTACT. THE FACE OF INNOCENCE BABIES WEAR IS PART OF THE EGO'S STRATEGY OF KEEPING US BELIEVING THAT WE ARE THE VICTIMS OF A WORLD BEING DONE TO US RATHER THAN BY US.

WHAA! PAY ATTENTION TO ME AND HONOR MY SPECIAL NEEDS!

NO EGO EQUALS NO INCARNATION.

NO = NO

BODIES HELP MAKE THE MIND MINDLESS: FIXATED ON THE ILLUSORY DREAM UNIVERSE. BODIES HELP KEEP THE MIND OBLIVIOUS OF ITS DECISION MAKING POWER TO CHOOSE THE HOLY SPIRIT OVER THE EGO.

KEEP YOUR ATTENTION EXTERNAL KID, AND I'LL GIVE YOU SOME CANDY.

WAKE UP.

AS WAS MENTIONED IN CHAPTER ONE NINTH, BODIES COME IN MANY FORMS. IN FACT, BODIES ARE FORMS: AN ATOM, A CELL, A PLANT, A PLANET, ARE ALL BODIES.

BODIES ARE MADE OF BODIES IN A KIND OF HIERARCHY OF BODIES. YET, WHETHER THEY ARE HOMO SAPIENS, SNAILS, SINGLE CELLS, ROCKS, OR ANY OTHER FORM OF BODY, ALL BODIES ARE EQUAL IN THEIR UNREALITY.

ALL BODIES ARE MERELY THE RESULT OF A SINGLE, REPEATED, PROJECTED THOUGHT: THE FRACTAL OF DUALISM.

SPLIT

BOND

1

THE FRACTAL OF DUALISM IS ALL ABOUT DIVISION, AND DIVISION MAKES INFORMATION. INFORMATION IS ARRANGED TO FORM VARIOUS **SPECIAL BONDS** THAT AT THEIR CORE MERELY ACT TO EMPHASIZE **SPECIAL DIFFERENCES**, AND THUS SEPARATION. IN THAT SENSE, THE WHOLE PHYSICAL UNIVERSE OF BODIES CAN BE DESCRIBED IN TERMS OF **INFORMATION**. BUT THAT SUBJECT IS BEYOND THE SCOPE OF THIS BOOK.

THE FRACTAL OF DUALISM IN A 4 BIT UNIVERSE

1111	1011	0000	0100
1110	1001	0001	0110
1101	1000	0010	0111
1100	1010	0011	0101

IT SUFFICES TO SAY THAT INFORMATION IS ESSENTIALLY **ENERGY**. AND THE FORMATION OF BODIES THROUGH SPECIAL BONDS IS A PROCESS THAT EXPENDS ENERGY. IN OTHER WORDS, TO MAKE BODIES, A PREEXISTING BOND MUST BREAK TO FORM A NEW BOND, AND THAT PROCESS EXPENDS ENERGY.

PROJECTED THOUGHT IS INFORMATION. AND A BODY IS LIKE A STRING OF INFORMATION. INFORMATION IS ENERGY AND HIGHLY CONCENTRATED ENERGY IS MATTER. THEREFORE, PROJECTED THOUGHT, INFORMATION, ENERGY, AND MATTER ARE ALL VARIOUS FORMS OF THE FRACTAL OF DUALISM.

ENERGY, WHICH IS REALLY JUST PROJECTED THOUGHT, CAN NEITHER BE CREATED NOR DESTROYED, BUT IT CAN CHANGE FORM.

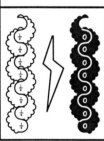

THAT'S WHAT IS SCIENTIFICALLY KNOWN AS **THE LAW OF CONSERVATION OF ENERGY.**

ENERGY IN THIS UNIVERSE IS A FEEBLE SUBSTITUTE FOR THE INFINITE ENERGY OF ONENESS: TRUE, UNDIVIDED LOVE.

THE PROCESS BY WHICH ENERGY CHANGES FORM IS CALLED WORK. OVER TIME, THE AMOUNT OF ENERGY AVAILABLE TO DO WORK IN A CLOSED SYSTEM DIMINISHES, WHICH INCREASES **ENTROPY**.

ICE MELTING IN A CUP IS A COMMON EXAMPLE OF **ENTROPY** IN ACTION. ENTROPY IS THE MEASURE OF THE AMOUNT OF ENERGY NOT AVAILABLE TO DO WORK IN A GIVEN SYSTEM. USING A SIMPLE **STIRLING ENGINE**, YOU CAN TRANSFORM INTO MOTION THE THERMAL ENERGY DIFFERENCE BETWEEN A CUP OF ICE AND ITS WARMER SURROUNDING ENVIRONMENT.

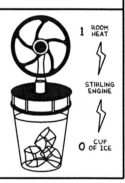

1 ROOM HEAT

STIRLING ENGINE

0 CUP OF ICE

WORK IS ESSENTIALLY WHAT MAINTAINS BODIES AND KEEPS THIS DREAM SEEMINGLY HELD TOGETHER.

BODIES REQUIRE DISEQUILIBRIUM. A BODY IN EQUILIBRIUM WITH ANOTHER BODY IS ONE BODY OR NO BODY.

ASHES TO ASHES DUST TO DUST

A CORPSE SEEKS EQUILIBRIUM WITH ITS ENVIRONMENT, WHETHER THAT ENVIRONMENT BE SOIL OR THE GUT OF AN ANIMAL.

FOR EXAMPLE, YOUR PHYSICAL BODY AS A WHOLE IS A TYPE OF SPECIAL BOND. YOU HAVE TO CONSUME OTHER BODIES TO MAINTAIN YOUR BODY'S METABOLISM. METABOLISM IS WHAT FACILITATES YOUR BODY'S DISEQUILIBRIUM WITH ITS ENVIRONMENT.

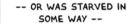
METABOLISM
* CYCLE MATERIAL IN
* EXTRACT ENERGY
* AND EXPEL WASTE

IF YOUR BODY BROKE IN SOME WAY --

THERE GOES MY HEAD.

-- OR WAS STARVED IN SOME WAY --

NO AIR, NO WATER, NO FOOD, NO HEAT.

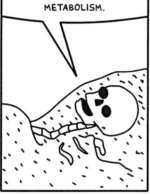

-- IT WOULD NO LONGER BE ABLE TO MAINTAIN DISEQUILIBRIUM WITH OTHER BODIES THROUGH METABOLISM.

CONSEQUENTLY, IT WOULD FALL APART AND BECOME **FOOD FOR WORMS** SO TO SPEAK.

THAT MAKES THIS A KILL OR BE KILLED UNIVERSE, WHERE GAIN IS DEPENDENT ON SACRIFICE.

EXAMPLE

TO EAT YOU HAVE TO SACRIFICE SOMETHING -- EVEN IF IT SIMPLY MEANS SACRIFICING A MUSHROOM.

IF YOU LIKE TO EAT A LOT, YOU USUALLY EITHER HAVE TO SACRIFICE HAVING A TRIM, AGILE FIGURE, OR YOU HAVE TO SACRIFICE BY EXERCISING.

IF YOU WANT A TRIM, AGILE FIGURE, YOU EITHER HAVE TO SACRIFICE BY EATING LESS OR BY EXERCISE.

THE EGO'S EDICT IS NO PAIN NO GAIN.

WHICH IS MERELY REFLECTIVE OF OUR FALSE BELIEFS ABOUT GOD: THAT GOD'S LOSS IS OUR GAIN.

IN PHYSICS, THE KILL OR BE KILLED PSYCHOLOGY BEHIND THIS UNIVERSE IS EXPRESSED AS **THE SECOND LAW OF THERMODYNAMICS** -- ALSO KNOWN AS **THE ARROW OF TIME.**

OUR EXPERIENCE OF TIME CORRESPONDS WITH SIN, GUILT, AND FEAR. SIN, GUILT, AND FEAR FORM THE UNHOLY TRINITY THAT GIVES RISE TO THE PAST, PRESENT, AND FUTURE THAT WE EXPERIENCE AS THE ARROW OF TIME.

TIME IS NOT REALLY LINEAR, AS THE ARROW OF TIME SUGGESTS, BUT DUE TO OUR GUILT, OUR EXPERIENCE OF TIME IS LINEAR.

AT NO SINGLE INSTANT DOES THIS UNIVERSE OF BODIES ACTUALLY EXIST; IT IS ALWAYS MERELY REMEMBERED OR ANTICIPATED.[5]

BUDDHA ONCE NOTED THAT:

IF THERE IS ONLY EMPTY SPACE, WITH NO SUNS NOR PLANETS (NO BODIES) IN IT, THEN SPACE LOSES ITS SUBSTANTIALITY.

AND SINCE SPACE AND TIME ARE INTERRELATED SEPARATION IDEAS, THE SAME CAN BE SAID OF TIME.

TIME AND SPACE ARE ONE ILLUSION OF SEPARATION, WHICH TAKES DIFFERENT FORMS.[6]

IF SEPARATION HAS BEEN PROJECTED BEYOND OUR MIND WE THINK OF IT AS **TIME**. [6]

I WONDER WHO WILL LIVE HERE 100 YEARS FROM NOW.

THE NEARER SEPARATION IS BROUGHT TO WHERE THE MIND SEEMINGLY IS, THE MORE WE THINK OF IT IN TERMS OF **SPACE**. [6]

I WONDER WHO IS AT THE DOOR.

DING DONG

SPACETIME APPLIED TO BODIES GIVES RISE TO THE **HUMPTY DUMPTY SYNDROME**.

AS YOU SHOULD KNOW, HUMPTY DUMPTY SAT ON A WALL. HUMPTY DUMPTY HAD A GREAT FALL. ALL THE KING'S HORSES AND ALL THE KING'S MEN COULDN'T PUT HUMPTY TOGETHER AGAIN.

THE IDEA OF A DESTROYED BODY, WHETHER IT BE AN EGG, A MUG, A DOG, A HUMAN, OR WHATEVER, REINFORCES THE EGO'S THOUGHT SYSTEM OF SIN, GUILT, AND FEAR.

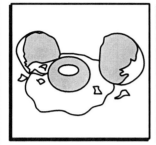  

SIN IS THE IDEA OF A **PAST** MISTAKE THAT CANNOT BE UNDONE.

HUMPTY FALLING OFF THE WALL.

GUILT IS THE **PRESENT** PERCEPTION OF THE REPERCUSSIONS STEMMING FROM THE PAST SIN.

HUMPTY IN FREE FALL.

AND FEAR IS THE **ANTICIPATION** OF PUNISHMENT.

HUMPTY DESTROYED WHEN HE HITS THE GROUND.

FORTUNATELY, MIND DOESN'T OPERATE UNDER THE SAME INSANE RULES AS BODIES. MIND IS ETERNAL, WHICH MEANS FRAGMENTS OF MIND ARE ALSO ETERNAL -- BUT NOT ETERNALLY FRAGMENTS.

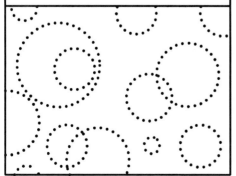

IN REALITY, THIS WHOLE DREAM HAS ALREADY **ENDED**, BECAUSE IT NEVER REALLY BEGAN. AND THAT FACT IS REPRESENTED BY THE HOLY SPIRIT'S ALTERNATIVE TO TIME CALLED THE **HOLY INSTANT**.

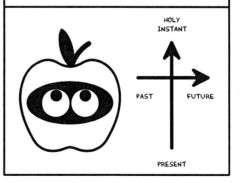

SPACETIME IS SOMETHING THAT MERELY SEEMS TO EXIST; IT CAN ONLY BE FOUND INSIDE THIS DREAM, NOT OUTSIDE OF IT.

THUS, SINCE THIS DREAM WAS MADE OUTSIDE OF ITSELF, THE SCRIPT OF THIS UNIVERSE HAS ALREADY BEEN WRITTEN. IT IS LIKE A **VIDEO GAME**. A VIDEO GAME IS PRE-WRITTEN, BUT THERE ARE MANY DIFFERENT WAYS TO GET TO THE END OF THE GAME.

AND LIKE PLAYERS OF A VIDEO GAME, WE ARE NOT ACTUALLY HERE IN THIS UNIVERSE RIGHT NOW. WE ARE INSTEAD ON A PRE-WRITTEN INFORMATIONAL BOUNDARY IN OUR ONE MIND FROM WHICH WE ARE REVIEWING THIS PROJECTED UNIVERSE.

WE ARE MERELY IMMERSIVELY THUMBING THROUGH THE PAGES OF AN ANCIENT TALE OF MADNESS, REFUSING TO PUT IT DOWN AND RETURN TO REALITY.

WHAT'S WRITTEN IN THE SCRIPT WILL HAPPEN, AND IN FACT ALREADY HAS HAPPENED, NO MATTER WHAT WE VAINLY TRY TO DO TO ALTER THE DREAM SCRIPT FROM WITHIN THIS DREAM.

WE ALREADY WROTE THE BEGINNING, THE MIDDLE, AND THE END. SO, ON AN UNCONSCIOUS LEVEL, WE ALREADY KNOW EVERYTHING IN THE SCRIPT.

DEATH DATES ARE DETERMINED, BIRTH DATES ARE DETERMINED, MORE DEATH DATES ARE DETERMINED, AND EVERYTHING IN BETWEEN.

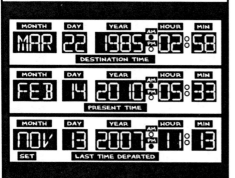

THERE ARE ALTERNATE SCENARIOS IN THE SCRIPT. BUT TO MERELY CHOOSE TO CONTINUE TO DREAM ONE VARIATION OF THE DREAM OVER ANOTHER IS A ZERO SUM GAME.

SHOULD I HAVE AN OREO COOKIE OR A CHOCOLATE CHIP?

THE ONLY TRUE FORM OF FREE WILL WE HAVE WITHIN THIS DREAM IS OUR ABILITY TO CHOOSE THE HOLY SPIRIT OVER THE EGO.

THE HOLY SPIRIT LOOKS BACK FROM THE END OF TIME TO LEAD US OUT OF THIS DREAM.

THEREFORE, THE MORE WE LET OUR REPRESSED RIGHT MIND (THE HOLY SPIRIT) BREAK THROUGH, THE SHORTER THE SCRIPT BECOMES.

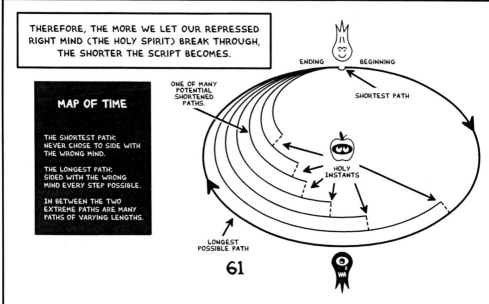

MAP OF TIME

THE SHORTEST PATH:
NEVER CHOSE TO SIDE WITH THE WRONG MIND.

THE LONGEST PATH:
SIDED WITH THE WRONG MIND EVERY STEP POSSIBLE.

IN BETWEEN THE TWO EXTREME PATHS ARE MANY PATHS OF VARYING LENGTHS.

ENDING   BEGINNING

ONE OF MANY POTENTIAL SHORTENED PATHS.

SHORTEST PATH

HOLY INSTANTS

LONGEST POSSIBLE PATH

61

AND THE SHORTER THE SCRIPT BECOMES, THE FASTER WE END THIS NIGHTMARE UNIVERSE.

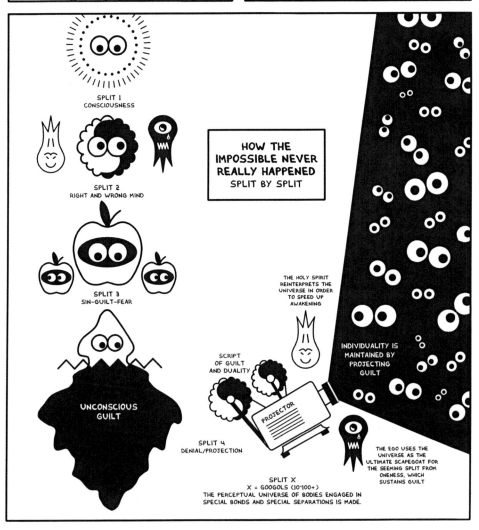

SPLIT 1
CONSCIOUSNESS

SPLIT 2
RIGHT AND WRONG MIND

SPLIT 3
SIN-GUILT-FEAR

UNCONSCIOUS GUILT

HOW THE IMPOSSIBLE NEVER REALLY HAPPENED
SPLIT BY SPLIT

THE HOLY SPIRIT REINTERPRETS THE UNIVERSE IN ORDER TO SPEED UP AWAKENING

INDIVIDUALITY IS MAINTAINED BY PROJECTING GUILT

SCRIPT OF GUILT AND DUALITY

PROJECTOR

SPLIT 4
DENIAL/PROJECTION

THE EGO USES THE UNIVERSE AS THE ULTIMATE SCAPEGOAT FOR THE SEEMING SPLIT FROM ONENESS, WHICH SUSTAINS GUILT

SPLIT X
X = GOOGOLS $(10 \hat{} 100+)$
THE PERCEPTUAL UNIVERSE OF BODIES ENGAGED IN SPECIAL BONDS AND SPECIAL SEPARATIONS IS MADE.

CHAPTER
FOUR NINTHS

THE EGO'S NIGHTMARE

WHEN WE SEEMINGLY DREAMT UP THIS IMPOSSIBLE UNIVERSE NEARLY 14 BILLION DREAM YEARS AGO, WE DID SO BY ESTABLISHING FIVE INSANE, CHAOTIC LAWS.

 ## THE LAWS OF CHAOS [1]
(ASTROPSYCHOSIS)

1 THE TRUTH IS DIFFERENT FOR EVERYONE. EVERYONE IS SEPARATE WITH SEPARATE SETS OF THOUGHTS AND VALUES. THERE ARE DEGREES OF TRUTH TO ILLUSIONS MAKING SOME SEEMINGLY MORE REAL AND UNCONQUERABLE THAN OTHERS.

2 EVERYONE MUST SIN, AND THEREFORE DESERVES ATTACK AND DEATH. ERRORS CALL FOR PUNISHMENT AND NOT CORRECTION. EVERYONE MUST PLACE AN IRREVOCABLE DEATH SENTENCE UPON HIMSELF, WHICH GOD IS POWERLESS TO OVERCOME.

3 GOD ACCEPTS THE SEPARATION WITH HATE, WHICH MAKES SALVATION IMPOSSIBLE.

4 KILL OR BE KILLED. GAIN IS DEPENDENT ON ANOTHER'S LOSS. EVERYONE HAS WHAT HE HAS TAKEN. AND WHAT HE HAS TAKEN IS VALUABLE BECAUSE HE KEEPS IT HIDDEN IN HIS BODY.

5 THERE IS A SUBSTITUTE FOR LOVE (SPECIALNESS) BORN OF STEALING FROM ANOTHER WHAT HE KEEPS HIDDEN IN HIS SPECIAL BODY.

THE LAWS OF CHAOS ARE COMPLETELY INSANE. YET, THEY ARE WHAT MAKE THE GROUND BENEATH OUR FEET SEEM SOLID. IF WE DIDN'T BELIEVE THE LAWS OF CHAOS, WE WOULDN'T THINK WE ARE HERE.

1 THE TRUTH IS DIFFERENT FOR EVERYONE. EVERYONE IS SEPARATE WITH SEPARATE SETS OF THOUGHTS AND VALUES. THERE ARE DEGREES OF TRUTH TO ILLUSIONS MAKING SOME SEEMINGLY MORE REAL AND UNCONQUERABLE THAN OTHERS. 2 EVERYONE MUST SIN, AND THEREFORE DESERVES ATTACK AND DEATH. ERRORS CALL FOR PUNISHMENT AND NOT CORRECTION. EVERYONE MUST PLACE AN IRREVOCABLE DEATH SENTENCE UPON HIMSELF, WHICH GOD IS POWERLESS TO OVERCOME. 3 GOD ACCEPTS THE SEPARATION WITH HATE, WHICH MAKES SALVATION IMPOSSIBLE. 4 KILL OR BE KILLED. GAIN IS DEPENDENT ON ANOTHER'S LOSS. EVERYONE HAS WHAT HE HAS TAKEN. AND WHAT HE HAS TAKEN IS VALUABLE BECAUSE HE KEEPS IT HIDDEN IN HIS BODY. 5 THERE IS A SUBSTITUTE FOR LOVE BORN OF STEALING FROM ANOTHER WHAT HE KEEPS HIDDEN IN HIS BODY.

DREAMS ARE BUT FORMS, THEIR CONTENT IS NEVER TRUE. BUT TO THOSE WHO LOOK ONLY UPON FORM AND DISREGARD CONTENT, THE LAWS OF CHAOS ARE THE LAWS OF ORDER. 2

THEREFORE, IF WE WANT TO CHOOSE THE HOLY SPIRIT AND AWAKEN FROM THIS DREAM, WE MUST EXPOSE THE CONTENT BEHIND THIS DREAM.

AND THE CONTENT BEHIND THIS DREAM IS THE EGO'S NIGHTMARE.

THE EGO EXISTS ONLY IN DREAMS. SO, THE EGO'S SURVIVAL DEPENDS ON OUR SLEEP.

THE EGO'S NIGHTMARE IS COMPLICATED AND CONTRADICTORY, BECAUSE IT IS FOUNDED UPON THE IDEA OF SEPARATION.

TRUTH HOWEVER, WHICH IS OF THE HOLY SPIRIT, IS SIMPLE AND CONSISTENT, BECAUSE IT IS FOUNDED UPON THE IDEA OF WHOLENESS.

THE TRUE PATH TO SALVATION IS THE RIGHT-MINDED PATH OF THE HOLY SPIRIT; IT LEADS TO WAKING UP.

THE FALSE PATH TO SALVATION IS THE WRONG-MINDED PATH OF THE EGO; IT SUSTAINS DREAMING.

SALVATION IS THE MEANS OF DEALING WITH THE GUILT STEMMING FROM THE SEEMING SEPARATION FROM GOD.

THE HOLY SPIRIT WANTS US TO MELT THE GUILT AWAY AND WAKE UP.

THE EGO WANTS US TO RECYCLE THE GUILT AND STAY AFRAID OF GOD SO THAT WE'LL REMAIN SELF-IDENTIFIED AS MINDLESS BODIES AND THUS CONTINUE DREAMING.

GUILT IS RECYCLED THROUGH DENIAL AND PROJECTION. THIS WHOLE UNIVERSE IS A PROJECTION OF OUR DENIED GUILT.

EVERYTHING SEEMS TO BE **EXTERNAL** TO US, EVEN OUR BODIES.

WHOA DUDE, LOOK AT MY HANDS.

IT IS SO WEIRD THAT I HAVE HANDS.

AND SINCE EVERYTHING SEEMS TO BE EXTERNAL, OUR **GUILT** SEEMS TO BE EXTERNAL TOO.

THE PROBLEM IS THE WORLD, NOT ME.

EXTERNALIZED GUILT TAKES THE FORM OF PROBLEMS. AND THE EGO DECEPTIVELY TELLS US THAT THE SOLUTIONS TO OUR PROBLEMS ARE ALSO EXTERNAL, WHICH KEEPS US FROM EVER REALLY LOOKING WITHIN TO THE TRUE ORIGIN AND SOLUTION TO ALL OUR SO-CALLED PROBLEMS.

UNIVERSE OF THE LIVING DEAD

THUS, LOOKING TO THE WORLD TO SOLVE PROBLEMS IS LIKE TRYING TO CHANGE A MOVIE AT A MOVIE THEATER BY BEATING ON THE SCREEN. THE SOURCE OF THE MOVIE IS THE PROJECTOR, NOT THE SCREEN. THE PROJECTOR PROJECTS A PRE-RECORDED FILM. YOU CAN'T CHANGE THE PRE-RECORDED FILM, ALL YOU CAN DO IS CHOOSE TO REMOVE IT FROM THE PROJECTOR AND REPLACE IT WITH PURE LIGHT.

ALEX AT MYSTERY SCIENCE THEATER

PROBLEMS KEEP US FOCUSED ON THE PHYSICAL AND THUS OUT OF OUR MINDS, OBLIVIOUS OF THE DECISION MAKING POWER OF OUR MINDS TO CHOOSE THE HOLY SPIRIT AND WAKE UP.

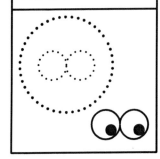

ALTHOUGH PROBLEMS COME IN COUNTLESS FORMS, IN TRUTH, WE ONLY HAVE ONE PROBLEM: THE GUILTY BELIEF THAT WE SEPARATED FROM GOD.

I ALREADY KNOW WHY YOU ARE HERE. YOU THINK YOU SEPARATED FROM GOD.

66

WE PERCEIVE A WORLD THAT IMPLICITLY TELLS US THAT WE'VE SEPARATED FROM GOD, FACILITATING IN US A PERSISTENT CONFUSION OF **IDENTITY**.

PERCEPTIHOLICS ANONYMOUS MEETING

HI, MY NAME IS ALEX AND I HAVE A PERCEPTUAL PROBLEM.

I FORGET MY SOURCE AND BELIEVE I CAN LOSE. I SEE ONLY ILLUSIONS: FORMS.

ALL THE OTHER PROBLEMS SEEMINGLY OUT THERE IN THIS UNIVERSE ARE MERELY SYMBOLIC OF THAT ROOT PROBLEM.

HEALTH PROBLEMS
ROMANCE PROBLEMS
FINANCE PROBLEMS
DRUG PROBLEMS
WEIGHT PROBLEMS
WORK PROBLEMS
SCHOOL PROBLEMS
TRANSPORTATION PROBLEMS
LEGAL PROBLEMS
FAMILY PROBLEMS

THEY ARE ALL PERCEPTUAL PROBLEMS STEMMING FROM THE PERCEIVED SEPARATION FROM GOD.

WHEN PROBLEMS ARISE, THEY BRING OUR **DENIED GUILT** OVER THE PERCEIVED SEPARATION FROM GOD TO THE SURFACE.

OH NO, MY CAR BROKE DOWN AND I DON'T LIKE IT; IT HURTS. THIS IS SUBCONSCIOUSLY REMINDING ME THAT I THINK I LOST GOD.

CLUNK CLUNK

THE EXPERIENCE OF GUILT IS THE SOURCE OF ALL FORMS OF **PAIN**, BOTH PHYSICAL AND PSYCHOLOGICAL.

GENUINE
ASPIRIN (A)
GUILT RELIEVER

325 MG

WONDERFUL DRUG

♡ FAST, SAFE GUILT SUPPRESSION

100 COATED TABLETS

THUS, THE THING THAT MAKES PROBLEMS PROBLEMS IS THAT THEY CONJURE UP GUILT IN THE MIND LEADING TO SOME FORM OF PAIN. WITHOUT PAIN, THEY WOULDN'T BE PROBLEMS.

GUILT GUILT GUILT GUILT

MY KNEE! EHHHHHHHHHH. AHHHHHHHHHHHHH. EHHHHHHHHHHHHH. AHHHHHHHHHH. EHHHHHH.

SO, IN REALITY, NO GUILT EQUALS NO PROBLEMS. **ALL PROBLEMS ARE PERCEPTUAL**. THE GUILTLESS MIND CANNOT SUFFER. [3]

WORLD TODAY
FIVE NEW THINGS THAT COULD KILL YOU

...ATE ON YESTERDAY'S
...THINGS THAT

HOWEVER, THERE IS NO GETTING RID OF GUILT FOR AS LONG AS THE EGO IS IN CONTROL.

THE EGO'S SEEMING EXISTENCE DEPENDS ON GUILT. THAT IS WHY THE EGO MADE THIS UNIVERSE AND MADE BODIES.

YOU SUFFER, THEREFORE I AM.

PEOPLE LIKE TO PRETEND THAT THIS UNIVERSE AND BODIES ARE NATURAL THINGS, BUT THEY ARE THE EPITOME OF UNNATURAL; THEIR FOUNDATION IS GUILT AND GUILT IS BY NO MEANS NATURAL. NATURE IS NOT REALLY NATURAL.

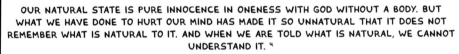

OUR NATURAL STATE IS PURE INNOCENCE IN ONENESS WITH GOD WITHOUT A BODY. BUT WHAT WE HAVE DONE TO HURT OUR MIND HAS MADE IT SO UNNATURAL THAT IT DOES NOT REMEMBER WHAT IS NATURAL TO IT. AND WHEN WE ARE TOLD WHAT IS NATURAL, WE CANNOT UNDERSTAND IT. [4]

ONENESS IS ALL THAT IS TRUE.

YEAH, I DON'T KNOW WHAT ONENESS IS. SO, WILL YOU JUST SHUT UP ABOUT THIS ONENESS CRAP ALREADY?

68

AS DREAMERS, OUR GUILT-LADEN IDENTIFICATION WITH THE BODY IS ALL WE UNDERSTAND. FOR THAT REASON, THE BODY IS THE **HERO** OF THIS DREAM AND THE HOME OF THE EGO; IT IS THE EGO'S IDOL. [5]

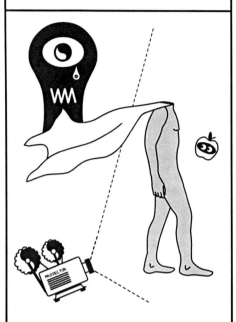

THE BODY IS THE BELIEF IN SIN MADE FLESH AND THEN PROJECTED OUTWARD. THIS PRODUCES WHAT SEEMS TO BE A WALL OF FLESH AROUND THE MIND, KEEPING IT PRISONER IN A TINY SPOT OF SPACE AND TIME, BEHOLDEN UNTO DEATH, AND GIVEN BUT AN INSTANT IN WHICH TO SIGH AND GRIEVE AND DIE IN HONOR OF ITS MASTER. [5]

THE EGO FEELS SAFE IN THE BODY BECAUSE THE VULNERABILITY OF THE BODY IS THE EGO'S BEST ARGUMENT THAT THE MIND SEEMINGLY INHABITING THE BODY CANNOT BE OF GOD. [6]

AND IT IS NO COINCIDENCE THAT ATHEIST LEANING PEOPLE COMMONLY USE THAT SAME ARGUMENT.

BUT THE EGO ALSO HATES THE BODY BECAUSE IT CANNOT ACCEPT IT AS GOOD ENOUGH TO BE ITS HOME. [6]

WE ARE TOLD BY THE EGO THAT WE ARE PART OF THE BODY AND THAT THE BODY IS OUR PROTECTOR, BUT THE EGO ALSO TELLS US THAT THE BODY CANNOT PROTECT US. [6]

HERE RESTS A BIG, STRONG BODY THAT POSED NO MATCH TO A BARRAGE OF BULLETS

SUCH A CONTRADICTION IS TYPICAL OF THE EGO'S INSANITY.

AND WE FALL FOR IT BECAUSE, INSTEAD OF TURNING TO THE HOLY SPIRIT, WE TURN TO THE EGO AND LET IT KEEP US DUMB AND UNAWARE.

REALLY? THAT IS WHAT I SHOULD DO? OKAY, THANKS BUDDY.

THE EGO WANTS US TO BELIEVE THAT WE ARE BODIES. THEREFORE, IT WANTS US TO BELIEVE THAT WE ARE THE EFFECT OF BODIES, AND CANNOT BE THEIR CAUSE.

UNDER THE COMMAND OF THE EGO, THE BODY TELLS THE STORY OF HOW IT WAS MADE BY BODIES, BORN INTO THIS UNIVERSE OUTSIDE THE BODY, LIVES A LITTLE WHILE AND DIES, TO BE UNITED IN THE DUST WITH OTHER BODIES DYING LIKE ITSELF. [7]

I AM JUST A SACK OF BLOOD. AND I CAME FROM OTHER SACKS OF BLOOD. SOMEDAY THIS SACK OF BLOOD WILL BURST AND THAT WILL BE IT.

IN THE BRIEF TIME ALLOTTED IT TO LIVE, THE BODY SEEKS FOR OTHER BODIES AS ITS FRIENDS AND ENEMIES. [7]

I WANT SOMETHING FROM YOU, YOU, AND YOU, BUT NOT YOU OR YOU.

ITS SAFETY IS ITS MAIN CONCERN. [7]

I SHOULD PUT ON SUN SCREEN.

ITS COMFORT IS ITS GUIDING RULE. [7]

I SHOULD TURN UP THE HEAT.

IT TRIES TO LOOK FOR PLEASURE, AND AVOID THE THINGS THAT WOULD BE HURTFUL. ⌐

ABOVE ALL, IT TRIES TO TEACH ITSELF ITS PAINS AND JOYS ARE DIFFERENT AND CAN BE TOLD APART. ⌐

THE DREAMING OF THE WORLD TAKES MANY FORMS, BECAUSE THE BODY SEEKS IN MANY WAYS TO PROVE IT IS AUTONOMOUS AND REAL. ⌐

THE BODY PUTS THINGS ON ITSELF THAT IT HAS BOUGHT WITH PAPER STRIPS, METAL DISCS, AND CREDITS THAT THE WORLD CALLS MONEY AND PROCLAIMS VALUABLE AND REAL. ⌐

THE BODY WORKS TO GET MONEY, DOING SENSELESS THINGS, AND TOSSES ITS MONEY AWAY FOR SENSELESS THINGS IT DOES NOT NEED AND DOES NOT EVEN WANT. ⌐

THE BODY HIRES OTHER BODIES, THAT THEY MAY PROTECT IT AND COLLECT MORE SENSELESS THINGS THAT IT CAN CALL ITS OWN. ⌐

71

THE BODY LOOKS ABOUT FOR SPECIAL BODIES THAT CAN SHARE ITS DREAM. [7]

HEY, YOU HAVE MY FAVORITE SKIN COLOR. WANT TO BE MY FRIEND?

SOMETIMES THE BODY DREAMS IT IS A CONQUEROR OF BODIES WEAKER THAN ITSELF. [7]

YOU BEST GET TO WORK BOY.

BUT IN SOME PHASES OF THE DREAM, IT IS THE SLAVE OF BODIES THAT WOULD HURT AND TORTURE IT. [7]

I COULD WORK BETTER IF YOU'D STOP WHIPPING ME.

THE BODY'S SERIAL ADVENTURES, FROM THE TIME OF BIRTH TO DYING, ARE THE THEME OF EVERY DREAM THE WORLD HAS EVER HAD. [7]

THE BODY IS **THE HERO OF THIS DREAM** AND NEITHER IT NOR ITS PURPOSE WILL EVER CHANGE. THOUGH THE DREAM ITSELF TAKES MANY FORMS, AND SEEMS TO SHOW A GREAT VARIETY OF PLACES AND EVENTS WHEREIN ITS **HERO** FINDS ITSELF, THE DREAM HAS BUT ONE PURPOSE, TAUGHT IN MANY WAYS. [7]

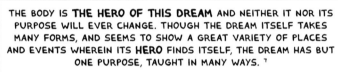

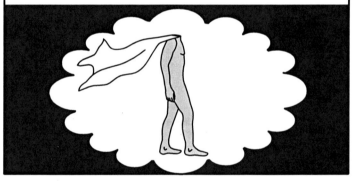

THIS SINGLE LESSON DOES IT TRY TO TEACH AGAIN, AND STILL AGAIN, AND YET ONCE MORE; THAT IT IS **CAUSE** AND NOT **EFFECT**. AND YOU ARE ITS EFFECT, AND CANNOT BE ITS CAUSE. [7]

YOU

IN TRUTH, THE BODY IS IN YOUR MIND. SO, YOUR MIND IS NOT IN YOUR BODY AS THE EGO CLAIMS.

REALLY, BODIES ARE MERELY **PUPPETS** MADE AND CONTROLLED BY A SCRIPT WRITTEN LONG AGO BY OUR ONE MIND.

SCRIPTED STRINGS, IN THE FORM OF SEEMINGLY EXTERNAL INFLUENCES, MANIPULATE OUR PUPPET BODIES.

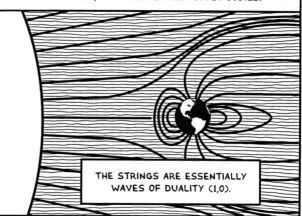

THE STRINGS ARE ESSENTIALLY WAVES OF DUALITY (1,0).

THE STRINGS CONTROL EVERYTHING -- EVEN OUR THOUGHTS.

BUT THE STRINGS ARE VERY COMPLEX, WHICH MAKES THEM HARD TO TRACE IN ANY COMPLETE SCIENTIFIC MANNER. THE STRINGS TWIST AND TANGLE IN A WEB OF DECEIT THAT KEEPS THE PUPPETEER HIDDEN.

THE ONLY TRUE FREEDOM OF CHOICE WE HAVE AT ANY GIVEN MOMENT WITHIN THIS SCRIPTED DREAM IS:

DO WE CHOOSE THE HOLY SPIRIT OR THE EGO AS OUR PUPPETEER?

THE PUPPETEER WE CHOOSE IS WHAT DETERMINES OUR SCRIPT...AND WHAT STRINGS ARE PULLED.

THE TWO SCRIPTS.

THE SCRIPT OF AWAKENING.

THE SCRIPT OF SLEEP.

THE MORE WE CHOOSE THE HOLY SPIRIT, THE QUICKER WE WAKE UP AND THUS STOP BELIEVING IN THE BODY AND THE DREAM.

CONVERSELY, THE MORE WE CHOOSE THE EGO, THE LONGER WE STAY STUCK DREAMING -- PLAYING THE EGO'S BODY-DEPENDENT GO NOWHERE GAME OF VICTIMS AND VICTIMIZERS.

THE GAME OF VICTIMS AND VICTIMIZERS IS HOW WE DEAL WITH OUR GUILT AND KEEP IT INTACT.

VICTIMS AND VICTIMIZERS

FOR ALL AGES

AN UP AND DOWN GAME FOR THE INSANE.

THE EGO IS ATTRACTED TO GUILT, BECAUSE GUILT IS THE WITNESS TO SIN THAT KEEPS US AFRAID OF GOD; GUILT IS OUR SELF-HATE THAT KEEPS US IN OUR DREAM STATE OF DIVIDED SELF-LIMITATION.

THE WAY THE EGO MAKES GUILT PALATABLE IS THROUGH PROJECTION.

IN THIS DREAM UNIVERSE, PROJECTION TAKES THE FORM OF SPECIAL RELATIONSHIPS.

SPECIAL RELATIONSHIPS

PROJECTOR

74

SPECIAL RELATIONSHIPS ARE THE HOME OF GUILT; THEY ARE USED IN AN EGO ATTEMPT TO SUBSTITUTE OUR RELATIONSHIP WITH GOD; THEY ARE A STRANGE AND UNNATURAL EGO DEVICE FOR JOINING HELL AND HEAVEN, AND MAKING THEM INDISTINGUISHABLE.

SPECIAL RELATIONSHIPS ARE A KIND OF UNION FROM WHICH UNION IS EXCLUDED; THEIR BASIS FOR THE ATTEMPT AT UNION RESTS ON EXCLUSION. [8]

SPECIAL RELATIONSHIPS EXIST WITHIN THE EGO'S FRAMEWORK OF SPACETIME; THEY DEPEND ON A PAST AND A FUTURE AND ARE TOTALLY MEANINGLESS WITHOUT BODIES. [9]

TO THE EGO, RELATIONSHIPS MEAN ONLY THAT BODIES ARE TOGETHER. THE EGO DOES NOT OBJECT WHERE THE MIND GOES OR WHAT IT THINKS. AS LONG AS THE BODY IS THERE TO RECEIVE ITS SACRIFICE, IT IS CONTENT. [10]

RECIPROCITY: YOU DELOUSE ME, I'LL DELOUSE YOU.

TO THE EGO, THE MIND IS PRIVATE, AND ONLY THE BODY CAN BE SHARED. TO THE EGO, IDEAS ARE BASICALLY OF NO CONCERN, EXCEPT AS THEY BRING THE BODY OF ANOTHER CLOSER OR FARTHER. AND IT IS IN THOSE TERMS THAT THE EGO EVALUATES IDEAS AS GOOD OR BAD. [10]

HEY BABE, I WISH YOUR BODY WAS HERE SO I DIDN'T HAVE TO TALK TO YOU.

WHAT MAKES PEOPLE GUILTY AND HOLDS THEM THROUGH GUILT IS **GOOD**. WHAT RELEASES THEM FROM GUILT IS **BAD**. [10]

NY TIMES BESTSELLER

THE SECRETS OF SPECIALNESS

HOW TO GUILT TRIP YOUR LOVE OBJECT INTO YOUR ARMS FOR LIFE

BY THE EGO

THAT PREFERENCE GIVES RISE TO THE EGO'S TWO FORMS OF SPECIAL RELATIONSHIPS: **SPECIAL HATE** RELATIONSHIPS AND **SPECIAL LOVE** RELATIONSHIPS.

SPECIAL HATE AND SPECIAL LOVE

WE USE SPECIAL HATE RELATIONSHIPS TO PROJECT OUR REPRESSED GUILT ONTO OTHERS. OUR ENEMIES ARE IN FACT VERY DEAR TO US, BECAUSE WITHOUT THEM WE WOULD HAVE NO SCAPEGOATS. WE GET TO PUT ON THE **FACE OF INNOCENCE** AND BLAME OUR ENEMIES FOR THE SEEMING DESTRUCTION OF HEAVEN.

WE USE SPECIAL LOVE RELATIONSHIPS IN AN ATTEMPT TO FILL THE INNER VOID LEFT BY OUR REPRESSED GUILT. OUR SPECIAL LOVES ARE VERY DEAR TO US BECAUSE WITHOUT THEM WE WOULD HAVE NOTHING WITH WHICH TO MASK THE **EMPTINESS** STEMMING FROM OUR GUILTY BELIEF THAT WE ARE SEPARATE FROM GOD.

YOUR FACE HERE?

SPECIAL LOVE IS WHAT PASSES FOR LOVE IN THIS WORLD. IT IS NOT TRUE LOVE, WHICH IS ALL-ENCOMPASSING, BUT IS INSTEAD MERELY THE EGO'S VERSION OF LOVE; IT IS A FEEBLE, FLEETING **SUBSTITUTE** FOR OUR HOLY RELATIONSHIP WITH GOD.

IN SPECIAL LOVE RELATIONSHIPS, PEOPLE BELIEVE THAT THEIR SPECIAL NEEDS ARE MET BY SPECIAL --

-- PEOPLE --

ROMANTIC PARTNER
FAMILY
FRIENDS
GENDER
GENERATION
ETHNIC GROUP

-- OBJECTS --

-- SUBSTANCES --

-- ACTIVITIES --

-- IDEOLOGIES, PLACES, AND SO ON THAT POSSESS **SPECIAL** ATTRIBUTES.

THE SAME THING APPLIES TO **SPECIAL HATE** RELATIONSHIPS: PEOPLE BELIEVE THAT SPECIAL PEOPLE, OBJECTS, SUBSTANCES, ACTIVITIES, PLACES, AND IDEOLOGIES ENTAIL GUILT AND THUS DESERVE ATTACK.

IT IS ALL VERY DISCRIMINATORY, JUDGMENTAL, ADDICTIVE, AND CHANGEABLE.

WHETHER SPECIAL LOVE OR HATE, IT IS ALL MOTIVATED BY **GUILT**.

A PSYCHOLOGICAL RULE OF THE MIND IS THAT IT IS IMPOSSIBLE TO LOVE SOMEONE WHOM YOU PERCEIVE AS DIFFERENT FROM YOURSELF. BECAUSE IF SOMEONE IS DIFFERENT FROM YOU, THEN THAT PERSON HAS SOMETHING YOU DON'T HAVE.

THE EGO TOLD ME THAT I'M INCOMPLETE AND THAT YOU, A SPECIAL PERSON, CAN COMPLETE ME.

SO, THE MERE ACT OF RECOGNIZING DIFFERENCES PRECLUDES TRUE LOVE. THAT IS BECAUSE TRUE LOVE IS ULTIMATELY NONDUALISTIC, WHICH MEANS IT IS SELF-LOVE. AND YOU CANNOT LOVE YOURSELF IF YOU SEE YOURSELF AS LACKING ANYTHING -- BECAUSE THAT ENTAILS DUALITY, WHICH IS PREDICATED ON THE BELIEF YOU ARE A BODY. LOVE MAKES NO COMPARISONS, ONLY SPECIALNESS DOES.

77

CONSEQUENTLY, SPECIAL LOVE RELATIONSHIPS AREN'T TRULY LOVE BUT ARE INSTEAD THIN VEILS OVER HATE; THEY ARE CANNIBALISTIC. IN AN INSANE AND FRUITLESS ATTEMPT AT COMPLETION, WE USE SPECIAL RELATIONSHIPS TO TRY TO STEAL BACK FROM OTHERS WHAT WE BELIEVE -- ON AN UNCONSCIOUS LEVEL -- THEY STOLE FROM US.

BALI MANGTHI KALI MA. SHAKTHI DEGI KALI MA, KALI MA... KALI MA... KALI MA, SHAKTHI DEH!

ALEX AS MOLA RAM

AND ONCE WE FEEL THAT THERE IS NOTHING LEFT TO STEAL, WE MOVE ON -- HAVING COMPLETED OUR SACRIFICE.

AH, YEAH, I THINK WE SHOULD SEE OTHER PEOPLE. I WANT TO START SEEING THIS GUY NAMED ALEX.

IT IS THE SAME DYNAMIC THAT GAVE RISE TO THIS DREAM UNIVERSE TO BEGIN WITH. BY ENTERTAINING THE IDEA OF SEPARATION, WE GOT THE IDEA THAT GOD WAS DIFFERENT FROM US AND THAT GOD HAD SOMETHING WE DIDN'T HAVE. THEREFORE, TO COMPENSATE FOR THAT LACK, WE TRIED TO STEAL FROM GOD WHAT WE FELT WE LACKED.

THE DANCE OF DEATH

TRUE LOVE IS CONTENT, NEVER FORM. THUS, SPECIAL LOVE IS A RITUAL OF FORM ONLY. THE DARK, HIDDEN CONTENT BEHIND SPECIAL LOVE IS THE SACRIFICE OF GOD, AND THUS THE SACRIFICE OF OUR TRUE SELF FOR FORM. AND ALTHOUGH YOU'D BE HARD PRESSED TO FIND A VALENTINE'S DAY CARD SAYING SO, SPECIAL LOVE IS REALLY THE DANCE OF DEATH.

IN THIS UNIVERSE, SPECIAL RELATIONSHIPS ON THE BODILY LEVEL ARE UNAVOIDABLE. EVEN THE BONDS THAT MAKE UP ATOMS ARE SPECIAL RELATIONSHIPS.

AS HUMANS, WE ARE BORN INTO A SPECIAL BODY THROUGH SPECIAL PEOPLE -- CALLED OUR PARENTS -- INTO A SPECIAL FAMILY.

WE GROW AND LIVE IN A SPECIAL PLACE AND A SPECIAL TIME, IN A SPECIAL CULTURE, UNDER THE RULE OF A SPECIAL GOVERNMENT.

TWENTY FIRST CENTURY AMERICA, BRAIN-DEAD CONSUMER CULTURE, CORPORATIST GOVERNMENT...

WE SPEAK A SPECIAL LANGUAGE, EAT SPECIAL FOODS, AND SPEND OUR DAYS DEALING WITH A VARIETY OF SPECIAL PEOPLE.

MID WESTERN ENGLISH, AMERICANIZED CUISINE...

THEN EVENTUALLY WE DIE.

BUT AFTER WE DIE, WE COME BACK TO REPEAT THE SAME SPECIAL RELATIONSHIPS AGAIN AND AGAIN IN ALTERNATE SET UPS IN ALTERNATE BODIES IN ALTERNATE SPACETIMES.

80

THE GAME OF VICTIMS AND VICTIMIZERS REPEATS AT EVERY LEVEL OF THIS DREAM. FROM CELLS, TO ANIMALS, TO NATIONS, TO GALAXIES, TO PLANTS, THERE IS AN EVER-PRESENT DUEL OF DUALISM.

THE DECEPTIVELY PEACEFUL SURFACE HIDES THE CONFLICT.

DUDE, WHY MUST YOU ALWAYS TRY TO STEAL MY RESOURCES?

IT IS NOT THE CIRCLE OF LIFE BUT THE VICIOUS CIRCLE OF GUILT.

AT ANY GIVEN MOMENT, IF ASKED, MOST PEOPLE WOULD CLAIM THAT THEY DON'T FEEL GUILTY.

I DON'T FEEL GUILTY. BUT I SURE DO HATE THIS, THAT, AND THEM.

AND THAT'S THE WHOLE POINT BEHIND PROJECTING THIS DREAM UNIVERSE; IT ALLOWS PEOPLE TO PROJECT THEIR GUILT ONTO OTHERS IN ORDER TO KEEP IT UNCONSCIOUS. WE LOVE TO SEE THE GUILT AND DARKNESS EVERYWHERE EXCEPT IN OURSELVES.

UP NEXT:
SPECIAL VICTIMS
A HIT TV SHOW THAT WILL ALLOW YOU TO PROJECT YOUR UNCONSCIOUS GUILT ONTO A FICTITIOUS CRIMINAL WHO, IN THE END, WILL BE PUNISHED.

LCD   PHONY

YET, DESPITE PROJECTION, PEOPLE STILL EXPERIENCE GUILT, BUT OFTEN CALL IT SOMETHING ELSE.

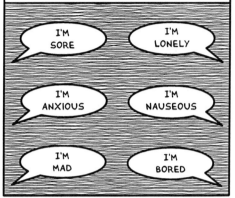

I'M SORE

I'M LONELY

I'M ANXIOUS

I'M NAUSEOUS

I'M MAD

I'M BORED

THAT IS BECAUSE PROJECTING GUILT IS A **RECYCLING** PROCESS. THERE IS NO ONE OUT THERE IN THIS DREAM THAT ISN'T ULTIMATELY YOU.

IN OTHER WORDS, AS YOU SEE OTHERS YOU WILL SEE YOURSELF.

YOU ARE A MORTAL BODY, I AM A MORTAL BODY.

YOU ARE IMMORTAL SPIRIT, I AM IMMORTAL SPIRIT.

YOU ARE GUILTY, I AM GUILTY.

YOU ARE INNOCENT, I AM INNOCENT.

WOULD YOU SEND MESSAGES OF HATRED AND ATTACK TO ANOTHER IF YOU UNDERSTOOD THAT YOU SEND THOSE MESSAGES TO YOURSELF? [11]

DEAR ALEX,

I HATE YOU.

HATE,
ALEX

OF COURSE YOU WOULDN'T. YOU'D DEAL WITH THE MESSAGES AT THEIR SOURCE AND SKIP THE EGO'S BLAME GAME OF PROJECTION.

THE BLAME GAME IS AN INSANE GAME, BECAUSE IT MERELY REINFORCES SELF-GUILT, ALBEIT ON AN UNCONSCIOUS LEVEL.

$ 6,000

Who is She? 5,999

$ 6,000

Who is he? 5,999

THE GUILTY ONE.

NO ONE WINS PLAYING THE EGO'S GAME. SO, DON'T FOOL YOURSELF. THE EGO'S GAME IS DUALISM.

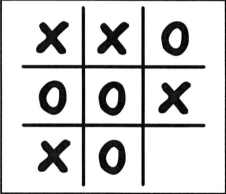

SURE, YOU MAY LUCK OUT FOR AWHILE AND FIND YOURSELF GOOD LOOKING TO THE SUBJECTIVE EYES OF THE BODY, WEALTHY, SURROUNDED BY GRATIFYING SPECIAL LOVE RELATIONSHIPS, FEELING SUPERIOR, LUCKY, AND NON-GUILTY.

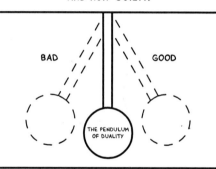

BAD

GOOD

THE PENDULUM OF DUALITY

BUT GIVE IT SOME TIME AND IT WILL ALL MOVE TO THE OPPOSITE -- IF NOT IN THIS LIFETIME THEN IN ANOTHER. THAT'S DUALITY FOR YOU. THE SO-CALLED GOOD AND THE BAD ARE JUST TWO SIDES OF THE SAME DUALISTIC COIN.

FRONT

DUALITY

JUDGMENT

IN GOOD WE TRUST

FRACTION

BACK

DUALITY

IN BAD WE DISTRUST

E UNUM PLURIBUS

THE BEAUTIFUL, CLOUDLESS, SUNNY DAY BECOMES THE DRY, SUN-BAKED, BARREN LANDSCAPE.

THE BEAUTIFUL, GENTLE, CLEANSING RAIN BECOMES THE FLOOD RAVAGED CITY.

THE BEAUTIFUL LITTLE PUPPY BECOMES THE OLD DYING DOG BEING PUT TO SLEEP.

THE BEAUTIFUL YOUNG WOMAN BECOMES THE OLD DECREPIT WOMAN.

84

THE FACT IS, THE EGO ACTUALLY WANTS TO KILL YOU, AND IF YOU IDENTIFY WITH IT, YOU MUST BELIEVE ITS GOAL IS YOURS. [12]

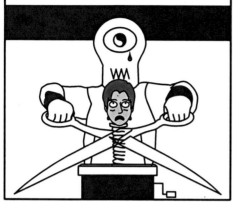

FORTUNATELY, YOU CANNOT REALLY DIE, AND SO THE EGO CANNOT REALLY KILL YOU.

YOU CAN PRETEND TO DIE THOUGH -- JUST AS YOU CAN PRETEND THAT SIN AND THUS GUILT ARE REAL.

TO THE EGO, THE EGO IS GOD, AND GUILTLESSNESS IS INTERPRETED BY THE EGO AS THE FINAL GUILT THAT FULLY JUSTIFIES MURDER. [13]

ANY FEARS YOU MAY EXPERIENCE IN CONNECTION WITH THE IDEAS IN THIS BOOK STEM ULTIMATELY FROM THE EGO'S INSANE INTERPRETATION OF GUILTLESSNESS. [13]

WHEN YOU CHALLENGE GUILT, YOU THREATEN THE EGO'S WHOLE DEFENSIVE SYSTEM TOO SERIOUSLY FOR IT TO BOTHER TO PRETEND IT IS YOUR **FRIEND**. [14]

HOLY SPIRIT!

HOLY SPIRIT!

BUT DON'T BE AFRAID OF THE EGO, BECAUSE THE EGO IS **NOTHING;** IT IS JUST YOUR OWN CRAZY, LITTLE, REPRESSED, SELF-HATING BELIEF ABOUT YOURSELF BASED ON THE FALSE AND IMPOSSIBLE IDEA THAT YOU DESTROYED HEAVEN.

GUILTLESSNESS IS THE ONLY THING THAT CAN TRULY PROTECT YOU. [15] AND FOR THAT REASON, YOU MUST LEARN TO TURN AWAY FROM THE EGO AND INSTEAD TURN TO THE HOLY SPIRIT.

HELLO ONENESS, MY OLD FRIEND...

YOUR **GUILTY SECRET** IS NOTHING, AND IF YOU WILL BUT BRING IT TO THE LIGHT, THE LIGHT WILL DISPEL IT. [16]

TO WAKE UP REQUIRES GIVING UP ONE THING --

-- GUILT.

BUT GUILT ISN'T REAL. THEREFORE, WAKING UP SIMPLY REQUIRES GIVING UP NOTHING FOR EVERYTHING. IT IS THE BEST DEAL EVER.

GOD™

PRICE: GUILT

THE IDEA OF GIVING UP SOMETHING IS A SACRIFICIAL CONCEPT AND THUS PART OF EGO DREAMING, NOT AWAKENING.

86

SO, DON'T MAKE THE MISTAKE OF THINKING THAT WAKING UP REQUIRES GIVING UP WHAT LITTLE YOU SEEMINGLY HAVE IN THIS DREAM.

AS LONG AS YOU THINK YOU HAVE TO GIVE UP SOMETHING, YOU ARE UNDER THE SACRIFICIAL SPELL OF THE EGO, AND THUS ASSIGNING REALITY TO GUILT. YOU CAN ONLY GIVE SOMETHING UP IF IT IS REAL TO YOU.

THE FEEBLE SUBSTITUTES FOR HEAVEN (**THE IDOLS**) THAT THIS DREAM OFFERS ARE ONLY VALUED BY THOSE WHO ARE LOST DREAMING OF GUILT.

TAKE AWAY THE GUILT AND THE IDOLS DISSOLVE INTO THE NOTHINGNESS THEY ALWAYS WERE.

GUILT IS NOTHING, AND GIVING UP NOTHING IS GIVING UP NOTHING.

AS YOU EASE OUT OF SLEEP, YOU'LL CONSISTENTLY BE GIVING UP MORE AND MORE OF NOTHING, WHICH IS AN EFFORTLESS AND JOYOUS PROCESS.

HOWEVER, TO THE EGO, THAT PROCESS IS QUITE TERRIFYING.

87

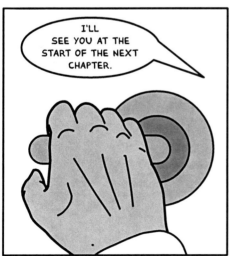

CHAPTER FIVE NINTHS

HAPPILY DREAMING AWAKE

SINCE WHAT KEEPS YOU, ME, AND EVERYONE ELSE ASLEEP IS GUILT, WAKING UP REQUIRES GETTING RID OF GUILT.

BUT THE EGO KEEPS OUR GUILT HIDDEN.

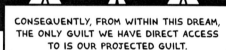

CONSEQUENTLY, FROM WITHIN THIS DREAM, THE ONLY GUILT WE HAVE DIRECT ACCESS TO IS OUR PROJECTED GUILT.

ZZZZIP

AND THEREIN RESTS THE SECRET TO WAKING UP.

THE SECRET TO WAKING UP IS --

DRUM ROLL

-- **FORGIVE** ALL THE GUILT PROJECTIONS THAT SHOW UP IN FRONT OF YOUR FACE.

IT IS THAT SIMPLE. **FORGIVENESS** IS THE ANTIDOTE FOR GUILT. FORGIVENESS MELTS AWAY GUILT.

HOWEVER, TO TRULY FORGIVE, YOU HAVE TO KNOW HOW TO FORGIVE TRULY.

SYMBOL FOR TRUE FORGIVENESS

SYMBOL FOR FAKE FORGIVENESS

NOT ALL FORGIVENESS IS THE SAME. THE EGO AND THE HOLY SPIRIT EACH HAVE THEIR OWN **BRANDS** OF FORGIVENESS.

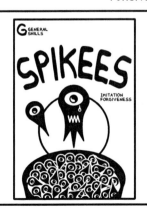

GENERAL SHILLS

SPIKEES

IMITATION FORGIVENESS

ONENESS

FORGIVEES

100% REAL FORGIVENESS

FREE THE UNIVERSE IS A DRUM STICKERS

THE **EGO'S** FORGIVENESS IS **FAKE** FORGIVENESS; IT KEEPS PEOPLE GUILTY AND ASLEEP; IT IS **FORGIVENESS TO DESTROY.**

91

THAT RIGHT THERE IS THE KEY TO WAKING UP, AND THUS THE KEY TO PEACE.

HOWEVER, PEACE ITSELF IS NOT THE GOAL. THE GOAL IS INSTEAD TO BECOME AWARE OF HOW MUCH YOU RESIST PEACE.

THERE ARE FOUR PRIMARY OBSTACLES TO OUR PEACE. [1]

OBSTACLES TO PEACE [1]

THE FIRST OBSTACLE TO OUR PEACE IS THE DESIRE TO GET RID OF PEACE, WHICH STEMS FROM OUR ATTRACTION TO **GUILT**.

THE SECOND OBSTACLE TO OUR PEACE IS THE BELIEF THE BODY IS VALUABLE FOR WHAT IT OFFERS, WHICH STEMS FROM OUR GUILTY ATTRACTION TO **PAIN**.

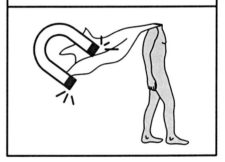

THE THIRD OBSTACLE TO OUR PEACE IS THE ATTRACTION TO **DEATH**, WHICH STEMS FROM OUR USE OF THE BODY AS A SYMBOL OF CORRUPTIBILITY.

REINCARNATE IN PERIL

AND THE FOURTH OBSTACLE TO OUR PEACE IS THE **FEAR OF GOD**, WHICH STEMS FROM OUR RELUCTANCE TO LIFT THE EGO'S VEIL OF GUILT THROUGH TRUE FORGIVENESS.

TRUE FORGIVENESS IS ESSENTIALLY
LUCID DREAMING; IT IS **NONDUALISTIC**
FORGIVENESS WHEREBY THE OBSERVER IS
THE OBSERVED AND THUS THE FORGIVER IS
THE FORGIVEE.

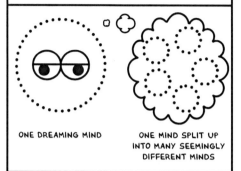

ONE DREAMING MIND

ONE MIND SPLIT UP
INTO MANY SEEMINGLY
DIFFERENT MINDS

YOU DON'T FORGIVE PEOPLE FOR WHAT
THEY DID. YOU FORGIVE YOURSELF
FOR BELIEVING A DREAM FULL OF
CHARACTERS THAT ONLY EVER DID WHAT
YOU ASKED THEM TO DO -- ALBEIT ON AN
UNCONSCIOUS LEVEL.

I MADE ALL THESE JERKS UP TO PROJECT MY OWN GUILT UPON.

WHEN YOU GO AROUND TRULY FORGIVING,
YOU GO AROUND SEEING THE DREAM AS A
DREAM.

REALITY IS UNAFFECTED BY ALL THIS.

YOU KEEP IN MIND THAT YOU MADE UP THE
DREAM.

THIS IS ALL **MY** DREAM.

YOU KEEP IN MIND THAT THE CONTENT OF THE DREAM IS MERELY SYMBOLIC OF THE
CONTENT OF YOUR MIND.

THE OBSCENE STUPIDITY I SEE IN YOU IS JUST A PROJECTION OF MY OWN BELIEF THAT I AM MYSELF OBSCENELY STUPID FOR THROWING AWAY HEAVEN.

YOU KEEP IN MIND THAT THE THINGS THE DREAM CHARACTERS DO AREN'T REAL AND HAVE NO CONSEQUENCE IN TRUTH.

THIS IS MY DREAM; IT ISN'T REAL.

YOU KEEP IN MIND THAT THE CHARACTERS IN THE DREAM ARE INNOCENT, IMMORTAL SPIRIT, NOT BODIES; THEY ARE ONE WITH YOU IN TRUTH -- DIFFERENCES ARE ILLUSIONS.

THESE PEOPLE ARE NOT BODIES; THEY ARE FREE, FOR THEY ARE ONE WITH ME.

THUS, OVERALL, YOU KEEP IN MIND YOUR RIGHT MIND, AND LOOK AT THE EGO WITH THE HOLY SPIRIT -- WHICH MOST OFTEN SIMPLY MEANS HONESTLY LOOKING AT YOUR RESISTANCE TO FORGIVE.

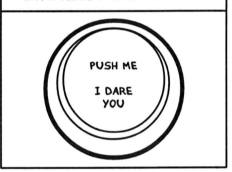

THE KEY TO PRACTICING TRUE FORGIVENESS IS VIGILANCE. WHENEVER YOUR BUTTONS ARE PUSHED, YOU NEED TO INTERCEPT YOUR HABITUAL, REACTIONARY **JUDGMENT** BEFORE YOU DISINTEGRATE INTO A TIRADE OF GUILT PROJECTION.

PUSH ME

I DARE YOU

IT TAKES MUCH MORE TIME AND ENERGY TO **JUDGE** THAN TO FORGIVE. TO FORGIVE YOU REALLY DON'T HAVE TO DO ANYTHING EXCEPT STEP BACK AND LOOK AT THE SITUATION WITH THE HOLY SPIRIT.

MAN, THIS GAVEL IS SURE HEAVY!

AT FIRST, IT TAKES SOME EFFORT TO STOP YOURSELF FROM REACTING, BUT EVENTUALLY YOU'LL DROP YOUR OLD HABIT OF AUTOMATICALLY JUDGING AND INSTEAD MAKE TRUE FORGIVENESS YOUR NEW HABIT.

YOUR MIND WILL SWITCH FROM A HABIT OF CONFLICT TO A HABIT OF PEACE.

WOULD I RATHER BE **HAPPY** AND FORGIVE?

OR

WOULD I RATHER BE **RIGHT** AND JUDGE TO JUSTIFY MY LACK OF FORGIVENESS?

AND BY THE WAY, AS A GENERAL RULE, ANY TIME YOU ARE TEMPTED TO REVERT TO THE EGO'S FAVORITE F WORD, YOU SHOULD INSTEAD CHOOSE THE OTHER F WORD, FORGIVE.

LOOK AT THIS OBLIVIOUS FORGIVEE ON HER CELL PHONE.

EVERY LITTLE THING THAT DISTURBS YOUR PEACE IN ANY WAY IS A REMINDER OF YOUR GUILT AND THUS A RELIVING OF THE SEEMING SEPARATION FROM GOD -- THE ATTACK ON TRUTH.

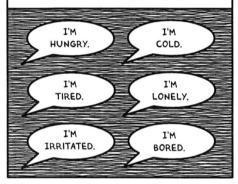

I'M HUNGRY.

I'M COLD.

I'M TIRED.

I'M LONELY.

I'M IRRITATED.

I'M BORED.

IN RELIVING THE SEEMING SEPARATION FROM GOD, YOU ARE ASKED TO CHOOSE ONCE AGAIN AND CHOOSE THE HOLY SPIRIT THIS TIME INSTEAD OF THE EGO.

THEREFORE, YOU MUST BE VIGILANT AND FORGIVE EVERY LITTLE THING THAT DISTURBS YOUR PEACE OF MIND.

BOOM BOOM PRRPP BOOM BOOM P BOOM BOOM PR

YOUR CAR AND MUSIC SUCK! YOU INCONSIDERATE DOUCHE!

WORLD TODAY

WHAT EVER HAPPENED TO MANNERS?

THAT IS HOW YOU MELT AWAY THE ICEBERG OF GUILT IN YOUR MIND.

95

YOU JUST HAVE TO REMEMBER TO **INTERCEPT** YOUR HABIT OF REACTIONARY JUDGMENT, CHOOSE THE HOLY SPIRIT, LOOK, AND FORGIVE; THEN THE HOLY SPIRIT WILL TAKE CARE OF THE REST -- ERADICATING THE GUILT IN YOUR MIND.

THE HOLY SPIRIT IS A SYMBOL OF THE RIGHT MIND, WHICH IS OUR TRUE SELF. YOU COULD INTERCHANGE THE HOLY SPIRIT WITH OTHER RIGHT-MINDED SYMBOLS, LIKE JESUS, BUDDHA, GUARDIAN ANGEL, **HIGHER** SELF, WHATEVER.

WE ARE ALL ONE IN OUR RIGHT MIND, SO ALL RIGHT-MINDED SYMBOLS ARE THE SAME AS LONG AS THEY RETAIN THE SAME CONTENT. IF YOU HAVE A PROBLEM WITH ANY ONE SYMBOL, FORGIVE IT.

I'M NOT REALLY THE CHARACTER MADE UP BY RELIGION. FORGIVE ME.

TURNING TO THE HOLY SPIRIT IS REMEMBERING YOUR TRUE SELF AND IT IS ESSENTIAL TO WAKING UP.

96

YOU CAN'T DO IT ALONE. TRYING TO DO IT ALONE IS WHAT MADE THIS DREAM TO BEGIN WITH. THAT IS THE EGO'S WAY.

LOOK! I CAN RIDE MY BIKE WITH NO HANDLE BARS.

TO BECOME A MASTER FORGIVER, YOU MUST REPLACE YOUR HABIT OF ALWAYS TURNING TO THE EGO WITH A HABIT OF ALWAYS TURNING TO THE HOLY SPIRIT.

SORRY EGO, I'M GOING TO LOOK AT THIS SITUATION DIFFERENTLY.

YOU'LL KNOW YOU ARE GETTING GOOD AT FORGIVENESS WHEN YOU START TO TURN TO THE HOLY SPIRIT AND FORGIVE EVEN IN YOUR NOCTURNAL DREAMS -- WHICH ARE PSYCHOLOGICALLY THE SAME AS YOUR WAKING DREAM.

OKAY HOLY SPIRIT, I'M TRYING TO WALK BUT MY LEGS WON'T WORK. SHOULD I TAKE THIS SERIOUSLY?

NOTE THAT NOCTURNAL DREAMS ARE PSYCHOLOGICALLY THE SAME AS THE UNIVERSAL DREAM. BOTH ARE ATTEMPTS AT FULFILLING A WISH IN OPPOSITION TO REALITY. THE ONLY DIFFERENCE BETWEEN THE TWO TYPES OF DREAMS IS THAT NIGHTTIME DREAMS ARE INDIVIDUALIZED AND THEREFORE HAVE LESS RIGID RULES.

AND IF YOU CAN EVEN REMEMBER TO FORGIVE IN YOUR NOCTURNAL DREAMS, YOU'LL ALSO REMEMBER TO FORGIVE EVEN IF YOU DIE.

OKAY HOLY SPIRIT, SOMETHING IS LIBERATING YET WEIRD HERE. SHOULD I TAKE THIS SERIOUSLY?

WAKING UP HAS NOTHING TO DO WITH DYING. SO, IF YOU DIE BEFORE YOU'VE MELTED AWAY ALL YOUR UNCONSCIOUS GUILT, YOU'LL END UP REINCARNATING.

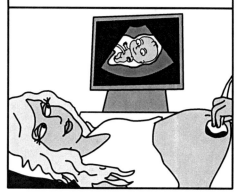

WHEN YOU DIE, YOU BRIEFLY BECOME FREE OF THE BODY. WHICH IS WHAT PEOPLE WHO HAVE NEAR-DEATH-EXPERIENCES REPORT.

HOWEVER, GUILTY MINDS DEMAND BODIES. SO, MOST MINDS CAN ONLY HANDLE A BRIEF INTERVAL OF TIME FREE OF THE BODY -- BECAUSE THE BODY IS THE HIDING PLACE FROM OUR UNCONSCIOUS GUILT.

AS LONG AS YOU PRACTICE TRUE FORGIVENESS IN THIS LIFETIME, YOU'LL ALREADY BE A NATURAL FORGIVER WHEN YOU ARE BORN INTO YOUR NEXT DREAM BODY AND LIFETIME.

WHICH IS TO SAY THAT THE DECISION MAKING PART OF YOUR MIND WILL NATURALLY BE MORE TUNED INTO THE HOLY SPIRIT.

AND YOU'LL RETAIN AN INNATE MEMORY OF THE THINGS YOU LEARNED IN THIS LIFETIME.

YOUR **BRAIN** DOESN'T REALLY KNOW OR REMEMBER ANYTHING; IT IS JUST A ROBOTIC PART OF THE DREAM THAT HELPS LIMIT MEMORY TO THE EGO'S SELF-SERVING, LINEAR NOTIONS OF SPACETIME.

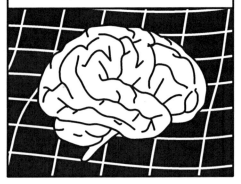

HOWEVER, UNLIKE YOUR BRAIN, YOUR **MIND** KNOWS AND REMEMBERS EVERYTHING; IT WROTE THE WHOLE SCRIPT OF THIS DREAM AFTER ALL.

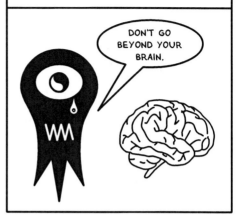

THE EGO KEEPS YOU DUMB AND FORGETFUL SO THAT IT CAN KEEP YOU ASLEEP.

DON'T GO BEYOND YOUR BRAIN.

THE HOLY SPIRIT HELPS YOU TO REMEMBER THE TRUTH SO THAT YOU CAN SWIFTLY AWAKEN.

DON'T TAKE THIS WORLD SERIOUSLY.

IF YOU PRACTICE FORGIVENESS, BUT DIE BEFORE YOU WAKE, YOU'LL FIND IN YOUR NEXT LIFE WHAT YOU NEED IN ORDER TO PICK UP WHERE YOU LEFT OFF. SO, DEATH IS NOTHING TO WORRY ABOUT.

IF YOU'LL LET THE HOLY SPIRIT TAKE CARE OF YOU, THE HOLY SPIRIT WILL TAKE CARE OF YOU.

IF YOU FAIL TO MELT AWAY ALL YOUR GUILT IN THIS LIFETIME, A HUNDRED YEARS FROM NOW YOU MIGHT READ THIS BOOK AGAIN IN SOME FORM.

AS TIME GOES BY...

PLAY IT AGAIN, EGO.

ALEX AS RICK BLAINE; CASABLANCA

99

NOTE: THE ILLUSION OF REINCARNATION ISN'T NECESSARILY CHRONOLOGICALLY LINEAR.

THEN EVENTUALLY YOU'LL BE ABLE TO LOOK WITHIN YOURSELF AND SEE NO LACK.

AT WHICH POINT YOU'LL BE ABLE TO EXTEND YOUR WHOLENESS BY JOINING WITH OTHERS, WHOLE AS YOURSELF. YOU'LL BE ABLE TO SEE BEYOND THE BODY AND THEREFORE SEE NO DIFFERENCES AND SO SEE NOTHING YOU WOULD TAKE FROM ANOTHER. [3]

I AM FILLED WITH AN ENDLESS SUPPLY OF LOVE.

CONSEQUENTLY, THROUGH FORGIVENESS, YOUR SPECIAL RELATIONSHIPS WILL EVENTUALLY BECOME HOLY RELATIONSHIPS.

HOLY LOVE SYMBOL

WHICH, IN OTHER WORDS, MEANS THAT IF YOU USE YOUR SPECIAL RELATIONSHIPS FOR THE HOLY PURPOSE OF FORGIVENESS, THEY'LL BECOME HOLY RELATIONSHIPS AND USHER IN TRUE LOVE.

I HAVE A BOYFRIEND AND HE'S NOT YOU.

THE SPECIAL LOVE OF THIS WORLD IS A FAR CRY FROM TRUE LOVE.

I'LL ONLY LOVE YOU AS LONG AS YOU MEET MY EXPECTATIONS.

UNLIKE TRUE LOVE, WHICH IS ALL ENCOMPASSING AND UNWAVERINGLY JOYFUL, SPECIAL LOVE IS VERY MUCH LIMITED, AND ONLY SEEMINGLY JOYFUL WHEN THE RIGHT SUBJECTIVE CONDITIONS ARE MET.

SPECIAL LOVE CONDITIONS AGREEMENT

BY SIGNING THIS YOU AGREE TO THE FOLLOWING CONDITIONS:

X

PREPARED BY EGO AND ASSOCIATES   PAGE 1 OF 19,475

WHEN THE RIGHT SUBJECTIVE CONDITIONS ARE NOT MET, SPECIAL LOVE RELATIONSHIPS OFTEN BECOME PAINFUL -- AND THE SECRET HATE BOILS TO THE SURFACE.

I KEEP ON FALLING IN AND OUT OF HATE WITH YOU.

YET, EVEN IF THE RIGHT SUBJECTIVE CONDITIONS ARE MET SUFFICIENTLY TO MAINTAIN SPECIAL LOVE IN A RELATIONSHIP FOR AN EXTENDED PERIOD OF TIME, BODILY LIFE IS ONE CONDITION THAT INEVITABLY FAILS.

DEATH OF A SPECIAL LOVED ONE BRINGS GUILT TO THE SURFACE. THAT IS WHY PEOPLE CRY OVER DEATH: THEY WEEP BUT FOR THEIR INNOCENCE. [4]

THIS IS THE INEVITABLE PRICE OF MY INDIVIDUALITY.

WITHOUT GUILT, THERE IS NOTHING TRULY SAD ABOUT THE DEATH OF A LOVED ONE.

NOTHING DIED, MERELY A CLASSROOM RAN ITS COURSE.

DEATH IS JUST NORMAL EGO TRICKERY. NO ONE EVER CAME HERE WITHOUT AGREEING TO THE SCRIPT AFTER ALL, AND THAT INCLUDES YOU.

THIS UNIVERSE IS THE **INSANE** PLACE WHERE THE **IMMORTAL** COME TO PRETEND TO DIE.

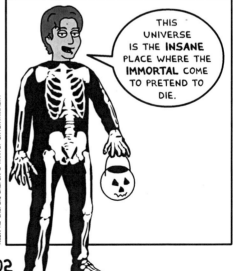

IF YOU PRACTICE TRUE FORGIVENESS, IT WILL HEAL THE UNCONSCIOUS GUILT IN YOUR MIND. AND AS A RESULT, YOU'LL BE EVER LESS PREOCCUPIED WITH DEATH.

YOU'LL BE WEARING YOUR BULLETPROOF VEST OF FORGIVENESS.

THEREFORE, YOU'LL BE ABLE TO CARE ABOUT PEOPLE ENOUGH TO REALIZE THAT THEY AREN'T BODIES, BUT ARE INSTEAD IMMORTAL SPIRIT AND FOREVER ONE WITH YOU IN TRUTH.

SO, IN OTHER WORDS, YOU'LL BE ABLE TO BE KIND TO PEOPLE WITHOUT JOINING IN THEIR SUFFERING.

SINCE BODIES ARE USED AS LIMITED COMMUNICATION TOOLS, WHEN PEOPLE DIE, IT SEEMS LIKE COMMUNICATION IS CUT OFF.

GET OUT

WHO SAID THAT?

HOWEVER, IN REALITY, ALL MINDS ARE JOINED. SO, DEATH DOESN'T REALLY BREAK COMMUNICATION ANY MORE THAN BODIES REALLY FACILITATE COMMUNICATION.

TRUE NONDUALISTIC FORGIVENESS IS THE ONLY TRUE EXPRESSION OF **LOVE** IN THIS DREAM. THEREFORE, TRUE NONDUALISTIC FORGIVENESS IS THE ONLY TRUE COMMUNICATION IN THIS DREAM.

YOU CAN FORGIVE PEOPLE AND THINGS WHETHER THEY ARE DEAD OR ALIVE, NEAR OR FAR.

103

AFTER ALL, THIS WHOLE DREAM IS ITSELF A MEMORY IN NEED OF FORGIVING. WE REVIEW THIS DREAM JUST LIKE WE REVIEW MEMORIES AND RECORDINGS OF LONG PAST PEOPLE AND THINGS.

IN THAT SENSE, THIS DREAM IS LIKE A SELF-MADE VIDEO GAME THAT WE REFUSE TO STOP PLAYING.

A PAINFUL MEMORY IS AN UNFORGIVEN MEMORY. AND EVERY MEMORY HARKENS BACK TO THAT **ORIGINAL** MEMORY WHEN WE SEEMINGLY SEPARATED FROM GOD AND **TERROR** TOOK THE PLACE OF LOVE. [5]

IN REALITY, THE SEPARATION IS OVER; IT HAS ALREADY BEEN CORRECTED.

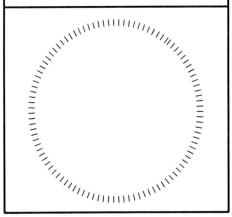

HOWEVER, WE CHOOSE TO KEEP THE MEMORY ALIVE AND SEEMINGLY REAL BY **RELIVING** IT IN THIS DREAM, WHICH, ACCORDING TO THE EGO, ATTESTS TO THE REALITY OF THE SEPARATION.

JUST FOR THE FUN OF IT, THINK OF ALL THE HORRORS IN THIS DREAM THAT CROSS YOUR MIND. THE SCARIER THE BETTER.

FOR EXAMPLE, SAY:

I AM AFRAID (FILL IN THE BLANK) WILL HAPPEN. [6]

104

YOUR THOUGHTS ON THIS LEVEL DON'T WRITE THE SCRIPT, SO DON'T BE **AFRAID** OF YOUR THOUGHTS.

SCARY THOUGHT
SCARY THOUGHT
SCARY THOUGHT
SCARY THOUGHT
SCARY THOUGHT

THE SCRIPT IS ALREADY WRITTEN, SO CHILL OUT. YOUR ONLY CHOICE IS BETWEEN THE EGO'S ELONGATED SCRIPT AND THE HOLY SPIRIT'S SHORTENED SCRIPT.

SCRIPT
SCRIPT

YOUR FEAR SIMPLY REPRESENTS YOUR UNCONSCIOUS GUILT. GUILT DEMANDS PUNISHMENT.

WITHOUT THAT GUILT IN YOUR MIND, YOUR FEARFUL THOUGHTS WOULD BE LAUGHABLE.

IMMORTAL + MORTAL = FUNNY.

ALL THOSE FEARFUL THOUGHTS ARE **ATTACKS** UPON YOURSELF; THEY ARE ATTACKS ON YOUR INVULNERABILITY.

NEGATIVE THINKING ISN'T NECESSARILY ANY DIFFERENT THAN POSITIVE THINKING. NEITHER ARE TRUE BECAUSE TRUTH IS ONENESS, NOT DUALITY.

WHEN THE EGO STRIKES, WHEN THE GUILT HURTS, WHEN YOU'RE FEELING BAD --

SIMPLY REMEMBER YOUR FAVORITE **ILLUSORY** THINGS, AND THEN YOU WON'T FEEL SO SAD.

DISTINGUISHING BETWEEN POSITIVE AND NEGATIVE IS A **JUDGMENT** THROUGH WHICH IT IS PRESUMED THAT SOME ILLUSIONS ARE GOOD AND SOME BAD.

FORGIVE THE SO-CALLED NEGATIVE AND ERADICATE IT. DON'T JUST TRY TO SUPPRESS IT WITH THE SO-CALLED POSITIVE.

IN TRUTH, ILLUSIONS ARE NEITHER GOOD NOR BAD, THEY ARE NOTHING. WHICH IS TO SAY THAT, TO THE HOLY SPIRIT, THIS DREAM UNIVERSE IS NEUTRAL.

THAT MEANS THAT WHEN SOMEONE TELLS YOU HOW SMART AND BEAUTIFUL YOU ARE, IT IS THE SAME AS WHEN SOMEONE TELLS YOU HOW DUMB AND UGLY YOU ARE. COMPLIMENTS AND INSULTS ARE EQUALLY **MEANINGLESS**; THEY ARE SUBJECTIVE JUDGMENTS THAT ALWAYS REFER TO ILLUSIONS: BODIES, PERSONALITIES, ETC. THEY ARE ALL JUST AN EGO SET-UP. THE TRUE YOU, **SPIRIT**, CANNOT BE COMPLIMENTED OR INSULTED BECAUSE IT IS PERFECT AND BEYOND DUALITY.

THE ONLY TRULY POSITIVE THOUGHT YOU CAN HAVE IN THIS DREAM IS THAT THIS DREAM IS **NOT** REAL.

NOTHING REAL CAN BE THREATENED, NOTHING UNREAL EXISTS. [15]

ALL OTHER THOUGHTS ARE TECHNICALLY DUALISTIC AND THUS ILLUSORY.

GOD DID NOT CREATE **NUCLEAR EXPLOSIONS**, AND SO THEY ARE NOT REAL.

GOD DID NOT CREATE CAR **WRECKS**, AND SO THEY ARE NOT REAL.

GOD DID NOT CREATE **EARTHQUAKES**, AND SO THEY ARE NOT REAL.

GOD DID NOT CREATE **DISEASES**, LIKE CANCER, AND SO THEY ARE NOT REAL.

GOD DID NOT CREATE ANY OF THE THINGS IN THIS FLEETING WORLD -- INCLUDING THE SUPPOSEDLY **GOOD** THINGS IN THIS WORLD.

THE ONLY THING GOD DID CREATE IS **YOU** -- YOU AS ABSTRACT SPIRIT.

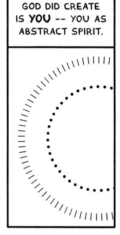

FOR THAT REASON, GOD IS IN EVERYTHING YOU SEE IN THIS WORLD, BECAUSE GOD IS IN YOUR MIND.

IF YOU SEE GOD AS FORGIVENESS, THE UNIVERSE IS UNREAL TO YOU.

IF YOU SEE GOD AS PUNISHER, THE UNIVERSE IS REAL TO YOU.

GET RID OF THE GUILT FROM YOUR MIND AND YOU'LL NO LONGER HAVE A WARPED, DUALISTIC VIEW OF GOD, OF YOURSELF, OR OF THE WORLD.

ALL FEAR IS FEAR OF GOD. IT IS THE DENIAL OF HOLY LOVE. FEARFUL THOUGHTS ARE JUST AS UNREAL WHETHER THEY PLAY OUT WITHIN THIS DREAM OR NOT.

THE EGO TRIES TO MINIMIZE FEAR BUT NOT UNDO IT. FEAR IS ESSENTIAL TO THE EGO'S GAME, JUST AS THE BODY IS ESSENTIAL TO THE EGO'S GAME.

EXAMPLES OF MINIMIZED FEAR:

BEING CONDESCENDING,
BEING UNBELIEVING,
BEING "LIGHTHEARTED,"
BEING DISTANT,
BEING EMOTIONALLY SHALLOW,
BEING CALLOUS,
BEING UNINVOLVED, AND
EVEN BEING DESPERATE. [16]

MOST FEARFUL THOUGHTS REVOLVE AROUND THE BODY. THAT IS BECAUSE THE BODY IS THE EGO'S PLOY TO MAKE YOU THINK YOU ARE VULNERABLE.

BUT REALLY, YOU ARE NOT A BODY, YOU ARE **FREE**. FOR YOU ARE STILL AS GOD CREATED YOU. [8]

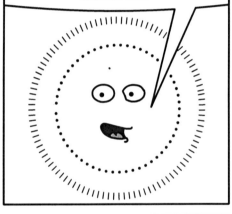

YOU HAVE SEEMINGLY DIED MANY TIMES. SO HAVE ALL THE PEOPLE YOU KNOW AND PETS AND EVERYONE ELSE.

YET, HERE YOU SEEMINGLY ARE TODAY AND SO ARE ALL THE PEOPLE YOU KNOW AND PETS AND EVERYONE ELSE. SO, DID DYING REALLY MATTER? DEATH IS MERELY A **MAGIC** TRICK TO FOOL MINDS MAD WITH GUILT.

MINDS **MAD** WITH GUILT ARE BOTH AFRAID OF DEATH AND ATTRACTED TO IT, BECAUSE BELIEF IN DEATH ATTESTS TO **MADNESS**. DEATH IS PRESUMED TO BE THE PUNISHMENT OF OBLIVION RESULTING FROM SIN; IT IS SEEN AS A KIND OF PENANCE THAT OFFERS AN ESCAPE FROM GUILT THROUGH SELF-ANNIHILATION.

WHAT, ME WORRY?

IN TRUTH, YOU, I, AND EVERYONE ELSE ARE ONE IMMORTAL SPIRIT, AND MIND IS THE CREATIVE ELEMENT OF THAT SPIRIT. THIS DREAM IS NOT LEFT BY DEATH BUT BY TRUTH. ⁹

YOUR BODY WILL SEEMINGLY DIE IN DUE TIME AND SO WILL THE BODIES OF EVERYONE YOU KNOW.

BUT THAT DOESN'T MATTER, BECAUSE YOU DON'T HAVE ONE LIFE TO LIVE; YOU HAVE AS MANY AS IT TAKES.

NOTHING TRULY LIVING CAN DIE: **MIND**.

AND NOTHING MORTAL CAN TRULY LIVE: **BODY**.

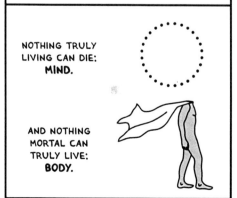

IF YOU WANT TO STAY IN DREAMS OF HELL LONGER, FOLLOW THE GUIDANCE OF THE EGO AND HAVE AN INSANE, BIPOLAR, GUILT-LADEN TIME OF AMBITIOUSLY SEEKING BUT NEVER REALLY FINDING.

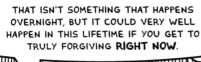

THE DESTRUCTION OF SOMETHING THAT ISN'T REAL DOESN'T JUSTIFY ANGER. [10]

TO Y'SHUA, THE CRUCIFIXION WAS NOTHING; IT WAS **PAINLESS** FOR HIM, BECAUSE HE HAD A **GUILTLESS MIND** INCAPABLE OF SUFFERING.

HE WAS LIKE:

OH, THIS IS WHAT THE SCRIPT CALLS FOR TODAY?

WHATEVER --

-- JUST ONE LAST USELESS JOURNEY.

THROUGH THE CRUCIFIXION, Y'SHUA TAUGHT ONLY **LOVE** FOR THAT IS WHAT HE WAS AND ALWAYS WILL BE. [11]

THE CRUCIFIXION WAS A CALL FOR **PEACE** AND NOTHING MORE.

TRUE LOVE HOLDS NO GRIEVANCES.

YOU WHO WERE CREATED BY LOVE LIKE ITSELF CAN HOLD NO GRIEVANCES AND KNOW YOUR SELF. [12]

TO HOLD A GRIEVANCE IS TO FORGET WHO YOU ARE. [12]

TO HOLD A GRIEVANCE IS TO SEE YOURSELF AS A BODY. [12]

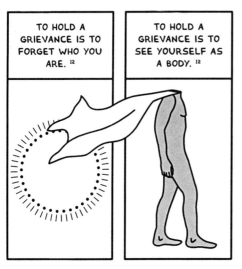

TO HOLD A GRIEVANCE IS TO LET THE EGO RULE YOUR MIND AND TO CONDEMN THE BODY TO DEATH. [12]

HOLDING GRIEVANCES SEEMS TO SPLIT YOU OFF FROM GOD AND MAKE YOU UNLIKE GOD. [12]

HOLDING GRIEVANCES MAKES YOU BELIEVE THAT GOD IS LIKE WHAT YOU THINK YOU HAVE BECOME, BECAUSE NO ONE CAN CONCEIVE OF HIS CREATOR AS UNLIKE HIMSELF. [12]

THUS, WHO CAN DREAM OF HATRED AND NOT FEAR GOD? [12] FORGIVENESS IS THE ANTIDOTE TO SUCH INSANITY, BECAUSE THOSE WHO TRULY FORGIVE HOLD NO GRIEVANCES. THEREFORE, THEY TRULY LOVE.

THERE ARE ONLY TWO EMOTIONS: **FEAR** AND **LOVE.**

ANYTHING THAT ISN'T AN EXPRESSION OF LOVE IS A CRY FOR LOVE, WHICH MEANS THAT EXPRESSIONS OF FEAR ARE JUST CRIES FOR LOVE. [13]

THEREFORE, THE APPROPRIATE RESPONSE TO EVERYTHING IS LOVE. THERE ARE NO COMPROMISES. LOVE IS REALLY SIMPLY LETTING GO OF FEAR.

INNOCENCE NEEDS NO DEFENSE. ANGER IS NEVER JUSTIFIED, ATTACK IS NEVER JUSTIFIED. SO, IF WAKING IS YOUR OBJECTIVE, DON'T FOOL YOURSELF THROUGH COMPROMISE.

ON THIS LEVEL, YOU ARE NOT RESPONSIBLE FOR WHAT OTHER PEOPLE DO, BUT YOU ARE RESPONSIBLE FOR YOUR REACTION TO WHAT OTHER PEOPLE DO.

SURE, IF SOME MENTALLY ILL PERSON IS GOING AROUND MURDERING PEOPLE, THAT PERSON SHOULD BE CAPTURED AND LOCKED UP TO QUELL THE EGO'S LURID SCRIPT OF VICTIMIZATION.

NEW KILLER LOOSE

...SAID HE WAS GOING OUT TO QUOTE, HUNT HUMANS.

BUT MURDER, LIKE ANY OTHER UNLOVING EXPRESSION, IS MERELY AN INSANE CRY FOR LOVE.

ALL FEAR AND NO LOVE MAKES JACK A SICK BOY.

DREAMS AREN'T REAL -- EVEN DREAMS OF MURDER. MURDER IS MERELY A SYMBOL OF BELIEF IN GUILT.

SO, YOU HAVE TO REALIZE THAT MURDERERS ARE JUST AS INNOCENT AS ANYONE ELSE IS.

113

THOUGHTS OF MURDER ARE PSYCHOLOGICALLY EQUAL TO SO-CALLED PHYSICAL MURDER. THEY ARE JUST SEEMINGLY DIFFERENT LEVELS OF DREAMING.

FORGIVE MURDERERS AND FORGIVE YOURSELF, BECAUSE MURDERERS ARE MERELY SYMBOLS OF YOUR OWN REPRESSED MURDEROUS THOUGHTS.

THAT IS THE KIND OF IDEA THAT THE EGO ABSOLUTELY HATES, BECAUSE IT **SUBVERTS** ITS WHOLE THOUGHT SYSTEM.

BUT SOMEONE HAS TO STEP UP AND HELP END THE INSANE CYCLE. IT TAKES TWO TO **TANGO** IN THIS DREAM. THEREFORE, FOR EVERY VICTIMIZER THERE HAS TO BE SOMEONE WHO AGREED TO BE A VICTIM.

REMEMBER, THE SCRIPT HAS ALREADY BEEN WRITTEN. NO ONE CAN BE A VICTIM IN THIS DREAM WITHOUT PREVIOUSLY AGREEING TO THE SCRIPT ON ANOTHER **LEVEL** OF THE MIND.

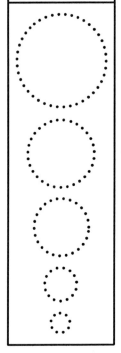

IN THE BIG PICTURE, THE IDEA OF AN INNOCENT VICTIM IS AN **OXYMORON**.

DON'T LISTEN. YOU HEAR ME?

THOSE WHO **ROBOTICALLY** FOLLOW THE GUIDANCE OF THE EGO CYCLE TROUGH AN ONGOING SCRIPT OF VICTIMIZING AND VICTIMIZATION.

THERE IS ALWAYS A SECRET AGREEMENT BETWEEN VICTIMS AND VICTIMIZERS BURIED IN THE UNCONSCIOUS.

IT IS WHAT PEOPLE CALL **KARMA**. WHAT GUILT GOES AROUND COMES AROUND. IT IS ALL A WISH TO KEEP SEPARATION SEEMINGLY REAL.

SO, DON'T BE SELECTIVE ABOUT WHAT YOU DEEM INNOCENT. ALL CONDEMNATION IS SELF-CONDEMNATION.

YOU ARE THE GUILTY ONE.

IF YOU ONLY WANT TO CALL CERTAIN THINGS INNOCENT, LIKE PUPPIES AND CHILDREN, BUT NOT ADULT HUMANS, INCLUDING MURDERERS, YOU ARE JUST FOOLING YOURSELF BY LOOKING ONLY UPON FORM AND NOT CONTENT.

BABY GROWS UP TO BE A MASS MURDERER

CUTE BABY = INNOCENT EXPRESSION OF LOVE

MASS MURDERER = INNOCENT CALL FOR LOVE

PEOPLE, ANIMALS, ALIENS, AND ALL BEINGS COME TO THIS UNIVERSE WITH GUILT BAGGAGE AND EGO INTACT. THAT IS WHY THEY COME; THEY MADE IT.

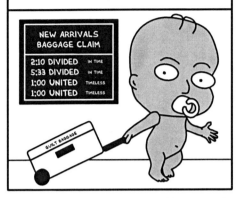

SELECTIVE FORGIVENESS WON'T GET YOU HOME, NOR WILL FAKE FORGIVENESS.

I ONLY LIKE THE MARSHMALLOWS IN FORGIVEES.

OTHERWISE, I PREFER SPIKEES.

BUT ALWAYS TRULY FORGIVING WITH THE HOLY SPIRIT **WILL** GET YOU HOME, BECAUSE IT WILL MELT AWAY THE ICEBERG OF GUILT THAT KEEPS YOU ASLEEP.

BY THINKING WITH THE HOLY SPIRIT, YOU'LL BE THE HOLY SPIRIT, WHICH IS YOUR TRUE SELF.

TRUE FORGIVENESS IS LIKE AN ADVANCED FORM OF **NONJUDGMENT**. THE EGO USES JUDGMENT TO DIFFERENTIATE BETWEEN THOSE WHO DESERVE TO BE HATED AND THOSE WHO DESERVE TO BE LOVED; THE EGO'S JUDGMENT IS ALWAYS BASED ON THE **PAST**.

THAT PERSON DESERVES SPECIAL LOVE AND THAT PERSON DESERVES SPECIAL HATE.

CONVERSELY, THE HOLY SPIRIT MERELY USES JUDGMENT TO DIFFERENTIATE BETWEEN EXPRESSIONS OF LOVE AND CALLS FOR LOVE; THE HOLY SPIRIT'S JUDGMENT IS ALWAYS BASED ON THE PRESENT: THE HOLY INSTANT KNOWN AS **NOW**.

THAT IS AN EXPRESSION OF LOVE AND THAT IS A CRY FOR LOVE. THE APPROPRIATE RESPONSE TO BOTH IS HOLY LOVE.

NONJUDGMENT IS WHAT BUDDHA USED TO AWAKEN, BUT IT DIDN'T GET HIM ALL THE WAY BACK HOME TO GOD -- AT LEAST NOT IMMEDIATELY.

THIS IS NEITHER GOOD NOR BAD.

NONJUDGMENT ALONE IS ACTUALLY MORE DIFFICULT THAN TRUE FORGIVENESS; IT TAKES LONGER AND DOESN'T DEAL WITH THE **GOD** ISSUE.

CONSEQUENTLY, BUDDHA HAD TO INCARNATE ONCE MORE TO REACH THE STATE THAT Y'SHUA WAS ABLE TO REACH USING FORGIVENESS.

JUDGE NOT LEST YE BE JUDGED, BECAUSE ALL JUDGMENT IS SELF-JUDGMENT.

INSTEAD, FORGIVE.

ALL SEEMING PROBLEMS IN LIFE ARE **LESSONS IN FORGIVENESS**. IF YOU LEARN THE LESSON AND FORGIVE, YOU WILL MELT AWAY THE GUILT IN YOUR MIND ASSOCIATED WITH THAT LESSON. THE RESULT WILL BE AN EVER MORE PEACEFUL AND JOYFUL MIND AS YOU RETURN TO YOUR NATURAL STATE OF ONENESS.

ALL MINDS ARE JOINED. THEREFORE, YOUR FORGIVENESS WILL TOUCH MANY PEOPLE YOU MAY NOT EVEN KNOW, AND SOMETIMES PRODUCE UNDREAMED OF CHANGES IN FORCES OF WHICH YOU WILL NOT EVEN BE AWARE. [14]

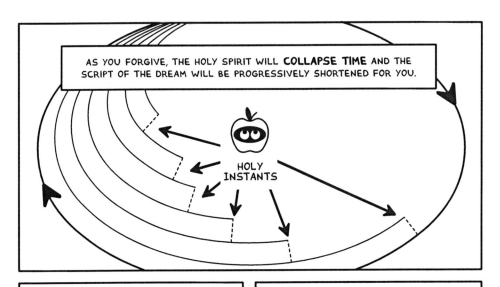

AS YOU FORGIVE, THE HOLY SPIRIT WILL **COLLAPSE TIME** AND THE SCRIPT OF THE DREAM WILL BE PROGRESSIVELY SHORTENED FOR YOU.

HOLY INSTANTS

BY TRULY FORGIVING, YOU'LL SAVE YOURSELF FROM MANY THOUSANDS OF YEARS OF EGO DRAMA MARKED BY MISERY AND TRAGEDY.

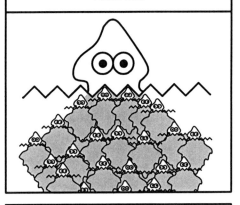

THAT IS BECAUSE FRAGMENTS OF GUILT IN YOUR MIND ARE DESTINED TO POP UP AGAIN AND AGAIN UNTIL THEY ARE FULLY FORGIVEN.

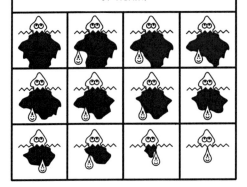

ONCE A GUILT FRAGMENT IS FULLY FORGIVEN, IT IS GONE, AND THE HOLY SPIRIT REMOVES THE PARTS OF THE SCRIPT WHERE THAT GUILT WOULD HAVE POPPED UP AGAIN.

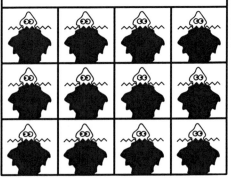

SO, WHENEVER YOU FIND YOURSELF RESISTANT TO FORGIVE SOMETHING, JUST ASK YOURSELF:

DO I WANT THE PAST REPEATED?

CHAPTER SIX NINTHS

TOTAL IMMORTAL

YOU ARE TOTALLY **IMMORTAL**. BUT THE EGO TRIES TO TELL YOU SOMETHING DIFFERENT.

THIS WORLD YOU SEE IS THE DELUSIONAL SYSTEM OF THOSE MADE MAD BY GUILT. [1]

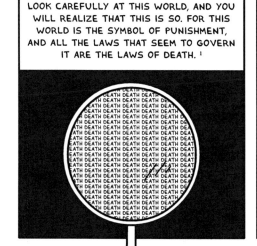

LOOK CAREFULLY AT THIS WORLD, AND YOU WILL REALIZE THAT THIS IS SO. FOR THIS WORLD IS THE SYMBOL OF PUNISHMENT, AND ALL THE LAWS THAT SEEM TO GOVERN IT ARE THE LAWS OF DEATH. [1]

CHILDREN ARE BORN INTO IT THROUGH PAIN AND IN PAIN. [1]

THEIR GROWTH IS ATTENDED BY SUFFERING, AND THEY LEARN OF SORROW AND SEPARATION AND DEATH. [1]

THEIR MINDS SEEM TO BE TRAPPED IN THEIR BRAIN, AND ITS POWERS TO DECLINE IF THEIR BODIES ARE HURT. [1]

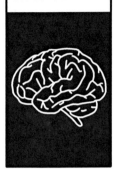

THEY SEEM TO LOVE, YET THEY DESERT AND ARE DESERTED. [1]

THEY APPEAR TO LOSE WHAT THEY LOVE, PERHAPS THE MOST INSANE BELIEF OF ALL. [1]

AND THEIR BODIES WITHER AND GASP AND ARE LAID IN THE GROUND, AND ARE NO MORE. [1]

IF THIS WERE THE **REAL WORLD**, GOD WOULD BE CRUEL. FOR NO FATHER COULD SUBJECT HIS CHILDREN TO THIS AS THE PRICE OF SALVATION AND BE LOVING. [2]

LOVE DOES NOT KILL TO SAVE. IF IT DID, ATTACK WOULD BE SALVATION, AND THAT IS THE EGO'S INTERPRETATION, NOT GOD'S. ONLY THE WORLD OF GUILT COULD DEMAND THIS, FOR ONLY THE GUILTY COULD CONCEIVE OF IT. [2]

THIS UNIVERSE IS A DREAM OF GUILT. AND FOR THAT REASON, BELIEF IN THE REALITY OF THE BODY IS ESSENTIAL TO THE EGO'S OBJECTIVE OF KEEPING US LOST IN DREAMS.

THE EGO WANTS US TO BE CONFUSED BETWEEN MIND AND BODY BY ASSIGNING MAGICAL ATTRIBUTES TO MATTER WHILE DENYING THE PRIMACY OF MIND -- BELIEVING MATTER MAKES MIND.

SPEECH CENTER   SMELL CENTER   HANDS CENTER   HEARING CENTER
REASONING CENTER   SELF DISCIPLINE CENTER
EMOTION CENTER   LANGUAGE CENTER
SPECIAL LOVE CENTER   VISION CENTER
SEXUAL CENTER
CENTER IDENTIFYING CENTER   KILLING CENTER   FANATICISM CENTER

SOME PEOPLE ADVOCATE THE BALANCING OF **MIND**, **BODY**, AND **SPIRIT**. BUT THAT IS A USEFUL OBJECTIVE ONLY IF YOU WANT TO STAY LOST HERE.

THAT IS EQUIVALENT TO EGO-IMPROVEMENT. YES, IMPROVING THE SUPERFICIAL EGO SELF HAS SOME PRACTICAL APPLICATION WITHIN THIS DREAM, BUT IT WON'T GET YOU ANYWHERE DIFFERENT THAN WHERE YOU ALREADY SEEMINGLY ARE.

THERE IS NO POINT IN REARRANGING THE DECK CHAIRS ON THE TITANIC, SO TO SPEAK.

WHAT YOU REALLY WANT TO DO IS USE YOUR **MIND** TO CHOOSE **SPIRIT** OVER THE BODY.

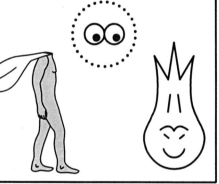

SINCE THE BODY IS THE EGO'S HOME, CHOOSING SPIRIT OVER THE BODY **UNDOES** THE EGO.

I'M MELTING, MELTING! OHHH, WHAT A WORLD, WHAT A WORLD!

ALEX AS A NA'VI: AVATAR

NO ONE EVER HAS BEEN OR EVER WILL TRULY BE IN A BODY. YET, THROUGHOUT THE COURSE OF THIS DREAM, WE HAVE ALL SEEMINGLY OCCUPIED MANY DIFFERENT BODIES OF MANY VARIETIES.

HUMANOID MANIFESTATIONS OF MIND TEND TO STICK WITH HUMANOID BODIES, JUST AS CANINE MANIFESTATIONS OF MIND TEND TO STICK WITH CANINE BODIES. BUT, IN THE BIG PICTURE, IT IS ALL NONETHELESS THE SAME **ONE** MIND.

121

SO, TO THINK THAT THE BODY YOU HAVE NOW IS ANYTHING SPECIAL IS TO BE DELUSIONAL. IN FACT, PEOPLE TEND TO BECOME WHAT THEY HATE FROM LIFE TO LIFE. THAT KEEPS THE EGO'S SCRIPT OF VICTIMS AND VICTIMIZERS ONGOING THROUGH ROLE REVERSAL. SO, BE CAREFUL WHAT YOU HATE, YOU JUST MIGHT BECOME IT.

OVERALL, BY COMPELLING US TO BELIEVE WE ARE BODIES, INSTEAD OF MINDS, THE EGO USES THE BODY TO KEEP US GUILTY, BELIEVING IN DEATH.

DEATH IN ITS PRACTICE FORM IS KNOWN AS **SICKNESS**. SICKNESS IS GUILT PROJECTED ONTO ONE'S OWN BODY.

PROJECTING GUILT ONTO OTHERS DOESN'T REALLY GET RID OF IT, BECAUSE, DESPITE THE EGO'S FALSE CLAIMS TO THE CONTRARY, IDEAS LEAVE NOT THEIR SOURCE. [3]

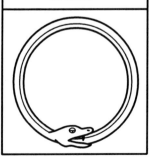

SO, INEVITABLY, IN ONE WAY OR ANOTHER, PEOPLE PROJECT GUILT ONTO THEMSELVES. AND THAT SELF-PROJECTED GUILT CAN MANIFEST IN ANY VARIETY OF PROBLEMS, FROM FINANCES, TO RELATIONSHIPS, TO LEGAL ISSUES, TO HEALTH.

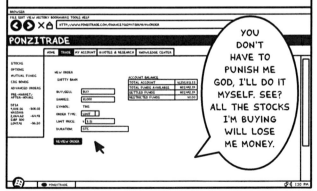

YET, WHATEVER THE FORM, EVEN SELF-PROJECTED GUILT IS FURTHER USED BY THE EGO TO PROJECT GUILT ONTO OTHERS.

SO, FOR EXAMPLE, A PERSON WHO GETS SICK HAS THE OPPORTUNITY TO PLAY THE **SACRIFICIAL VICTIM** AND BLAME OUTSIDE FACTORS ON THE SICKNESS, LIKE VIRUSES, HEREDITY, PARASITES, BAD LUCK, NEGLIGENCE, WHATEVER.

WHEN IT IS UNDERSTOOD THAT THE MIND, THE ONLY LEVEL OF CREATION, CANNOT CREATE BEYOND ITSELF, NEITHER TYPE OF CONFUSION NEED OCCUR. [4]

YET, EVEN THOUGH SICKNESS IS ULTIMATELY A RESPONSE TO MISTHOUGHT, ANY ILLNESS IS JUST PART OF THE PRE-WRITTEN SCRIPT.

SO, IF YOU GET SICK, CERTAINLY DON'T FEEL GUILTY ABOUT IT. GUILT IS, AFTER ALL, THE PROBLEM TO BEGIN WITH.

WHAT MAKES ANY ILLNESS A PROBLEM IS THAT IT IS ACCOMPANIED BY PAIN. NO PAIN EQUALS NO PROBLEM. AND NO GUILT EQUALS NO PAIN.

I'M SICK BUT I HAVE NO PAIN! SO, WHO CARES?

SO, IF YOU REALLY WANT TO MAKE YOURSELF IMPERVIOUS TO ILLNESS, YOU HAVE TO GET RID OF ALL YOUR GUILT. THAT MEANS YOU HAVE TO FORGIVE.

FORGIVING MEANS NOT ONLY FORGIVING YOUR OWN SEEMING ILLNESSES, BUT IT ALSO MEANS FORGIVING OTHER PEOPLE'S SEEMING ILLNESSES.

AND THAT IS DONE BY RECOGNIZING THE INHERENT INNOCENCE IN OTHERS AND THUS IN YOURSELF.

THAT IS ACTUALLY HOW Y'SHUA WAS ABLE TO HEAL PEOPLE. HIS OWN GUILTLESS MIND WAS ABLE TO SEE THE **INNOCENCE** IN OTHERS. THUS, HE DIDN'T SEE ANYONE AS ACTUALLY SICK. AND SINCE ALL MINDS ARE JOINED, HIS RECOGNITION OF INNOCENCE RUBBED OFF ON HIS PATIENTS, ALLOWING THEM TO CHOOSE INNOCENCE OVER GUILT.

YOUR SINS ARE FORGIVEN BECAUSE THEY ARE IMPOSSIBLE. YOU ARE SPIRIT WHOLE AND INNOCENT.

THE FACT IS THAT THE **SANE** MIND CANNOT CONCEIVE OF ILLNESS BECAUSE IT CANNOT CONCEIVE OF ATTACKING ANYONE OR ANYTHING. [5]

IT MUST BE UNDERSTOOD THAT WE ARE ALL HAPPY TO BE MISERABLE, BECAUSE OUR MISERY ATTESTS TO SOMEBODY'S GUILT. THAT IS HOW THE INSANE MIND THINKS.

NONETHELESS, JUST BECAUSE SICKNESS IS OF THE MIND, WHICH MEANS THAT THE MIND IS THE TRUE PHYSICIAN, THAT CERTAINLY DOESN'T MEAN A PERSON SHOULDN'T SEEK MEDICAL HELP FOR AN ILLNESS.

IF, FOR INSTANCE, YOUR FINGER GETS CUT OFF, YOU SHOULD HAVE IT SEWN BACK ON.

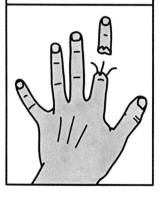

THAT IS HOW THINGS WORK IN THIS UNIVERSE. SEWING A FINGER BACK ON IS SYMBOLIC OF HEALING THE SEEMING SEPARATION FROM GOD. IF YOU HAVE IT SEWN BACK ON FORGIVINGLY, IT SHOULD BE ABLE TO HEAL.

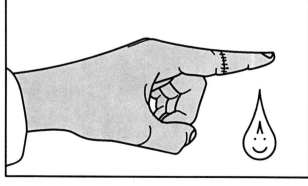

SICKNESS TAKES MANY FORMS, AND SO DOES UNFORGIVENESS. THE FORMS OF ONE BUT REPRODUCE THE FORMS OF THE OTHER, FOR THEY ARE THE SAME ILLUSION. [6]

I'VE LOST MY VOICE.

A CAREFUL STUDY OF THE FORM A SICKNESS TAKES WILL POINT QUITE CLEARLY TO THE FORM OF UNFORGIVENESS THAT IT REPRESENTS. [6]

WHAT IS THE PURPOSE OF THIS?

YET, SEEING THIS WILL NOT EFFECT A CURE. [6]

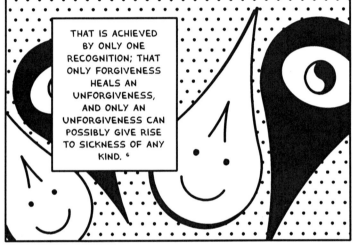

THAT IS ACHIEVED BY ONLY ONE RECOGNITION; THAT ONLY FORGIVENESS HEALS AN UNFORGIVENESS, AND ONLY AN UNFORGIVENESS CAN POSSIBLY GIVE RISE TO SICKNESS OF ANY KIND. [6]

SO, ULTIMATELY, PHYSICAL REMEDIES ARE JUST PLACEBOS. THAT IS WHY THERE IS SUCH A THING AS THE PLACEBO EFFECT. EVEN HOPELESSLY MATERIALISTIC SCIENCE CAN'T DENY THE PLACEBO EFFECT.

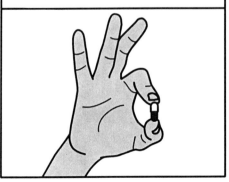

THE PLACEBO EFFECT IS A MAGIC TRICK THAT MAKES FORGIVENESS PALATABLE WITHIN THE EGO'S FRAMEWORK OF BELIEVING THAT SOMETHING OTHER THAN THE MIND CAN BE AT THE LEVEL OF CAUSE.

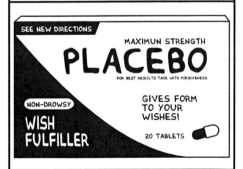

SEE NEW DIRECTIONS

MAXIMUN STRENGTH

PLACEBO

FOR BEST RESULTS TAKE WITH FORGIVENESS

NON-DROWSY

WISH FULFILLER

GIVES FORM TO YOUR WISHES!

20 TABLETS

126

WITHOUT THE HELP OF FORGIVENESS, PHYSICAL REMEDIES ARE JUST EGO MEDICINE. EGO MEDICINE FIXES ONE THING AT THE PRICE OF A NEW PROBLEM; IT IS A NO WIN GAME THAT JUST SHIFTS AROUND GUILT WITHOUT ERADICATING IT.

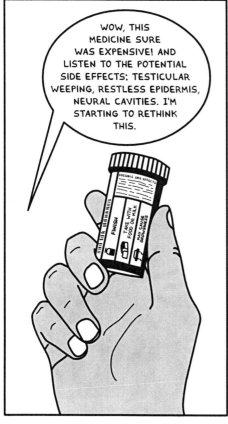

WOW, THIS MEDICINE SURE WAS EXPENSIVE! AND LISTEN TO THE POTENTIAL SIDE EFFECTS: TESTICULAR WEEPING, RESTLESS EPIDERMIS, NEURAL CAVITIES. I'M STARTING TO RETHINK THIS.

YOU CAN ONLY WIN PLAYING THE HOLY SPIRIT'S GAME OF FORGIVENESS.

FORGIVENESS WILL MAKE YOU GUILTLESS AND GUILTLESSNESS WILL MAKE YOU PAINLESS. IN THAT SENSE, FORGIVENESS IS LIKE FOOLPROOF HEALTH INSURANCE. THE ONLY COST IS THE EGO, WHICH IS NOTHING.

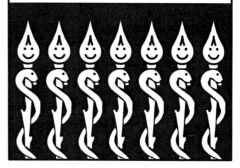

MOST PEOPLE WOULD LITERALLY FREAK OUT IF THEY WERE SPONTANEOUSLY HEALED -- JUST AS MOST PEOPLE WOULD LITERALLY FREAK OUT IF THEY WERE SPONTANEOUSLY TRANSPORTED THROUGH SPACETIME WITHOUT DOING SOMETHING LIKE WALKING, OR RIDING IN A VEHICLE.

LORD, HEAL THIS DEAF CRIPPLE!

IN THE NAME OF JESUS THROW DOWN THY CRUTCHES AND SAY BABY!

CAN YOU SAY BABY? SAY IT, SAY BAAAYYBEEE!

≥BANG≥

BAAAYYBEEEE!

THE EGO IS TOO MUCH IN CONTROL TO PERMIT SUCH THINGS FOR MOST PEOPLE; IT WOULD TOO DRAMATICALLY SUBVERT THE EGO'S THOUGHT SYSTEM AND BRING THE FEAR OF GOD STRAIGHT TO THE SURFACE.

NOTE: A FLIGHT INTO HEALTH CAN SERVE THE EGO'S PURPOSES IF THE ILLNESS IS BEING USED AGAINST THE EGO AS A MEANS OF LOOKING AT THE EGO.

THAT'S THE SAME REASON WHY THE HOLY SPIRIT HASN'T SHOWN UP SYMBOLICALLY TO ANNOUNCE TO THE WHOLE WORLD THAT THIS UNIVERSE IS ALL A DREAM.

ATTENTION EVERYONE, LOOK INTO THE SKY AND LISTEN TO ME. THIS UNIVERSE IS A DREAM.

AND THAT IS ALSO THE REASON WHY MOST PEOPLE DON'T LITERALLY HEAR THE VOICE OF THE HOLY SPIRIT IN THEIR MINDS IN ANY WAY DISCERNIBLE IN FORM FROM THE VOICE OF THE EGO.

HEY.

HEY.

ONLY THE CONTENT IS EVER DISCERNIBLE.

THEY ARE GUILTY.

NO ONE IS GUILTY.

NOTE: THE EGO ALWAYS SPEAKS FIRST. THE HOLY SPIRIT MERELY SPEAKS TO CORRECT THE EGO.

THE HOLY SPIRIT HAS TO SHOW UP TO PEOPLE IN FORMS THAT THEY ARE READY TO ACCEPT.

CONSEQUENTLY, THE HOLY SPIRIT ONLY SHOWS UP TO MOST PEOPLE IN MUNDANE AND WATERED DOWN FORMS, BECAUSE THAT IS ALL MOST PEOPLE ARE READY TO ACCEPT.

ALL YOU NEED IS LOVE. ALL YOU NEED IS LOVE.

THINGS LIKE WHAT YOU ARE READING RIGHT NOW ARE WHAT THE HOLY SPIRIT USES FOR PEOPLE WHO ARE READY FOR A MORE DIRECT DOSE OF TRUTH.

THIS BOOK'S FORM IS WITHIN THE NORMAL MEANS PERMISSIBLE BY THE EGO, BUT ITS CONTENT ISN'T.

THIS BOOK IS LIKE AN INTRODUCTION TO **MIRACLES**.

MIRACLE SYMBOL

MIRACLES ARE OF THE MIND; THEY ARE **SHIFTS IN PERCEPTION** THAT PUT MIND AT THE LEVEL OF CAUSE RATHER THAN EFFECT. MIRACLES ARE THE EXTENDING OF FORGIVENESS.

CAUSE

EFFECT

IF YOU WANT TO PERFORM MIRACLES, LEARN TO LOOK AT THIS WORLD AS THE DREAM IT IS AND TRULY FORGIVE WITH THE HOLY SPIRIT.

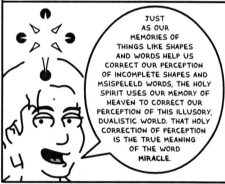

JUST AS OUR MEMORIES OF THINGS LIKE SHAPES AND WORDS HELP US CORRECT OUR PERCEPTION OF INCOMPLETE SHAPES AND MSISPELELD WORDS, THE HOLY SPIRIT USES OUR MEMORY OF HEAVEN TO CORRECT OUR PERCEPTION OF THIS ILLUSORY, DUALISTIC WORLD. THAT HOLY CORRECTION OF PERCEPTION IS THE TRUE MEANING OF THE WORD **MIRACLE**.

A MIRACLE IS NOT SURVIVING A PLANE CRASH OR A HEART ATTACK --

-- NOR IS IT DOING THINGS LIKE WALKING ON WATER.

A MIRACLE IS THE RECOGNITION THAT PLANE CRASHES, HEART ATTACKS, AND WATER AREN'T REAL, BECAUSE GOD DIDN'T CREATE THEM. A MIRACLE IS AN ACT OF UNPROJECTION.

PROJECTOR

FACE IT, BODIES DIE. THEY DIE IN MANY DIFFERENT WAYS AND AT MANY DIFFERENT AGES. THERE IS NO SUCH THING AS A SPIRITUAL **FORM** OF DYING.

HOWEVER, IF YOU USE YOUR TIME IN YOUR BODY TO FORGIVE, YOU'LL EVENTUALLY WAKE UP.

THEN, NO MATTER WHEN OR HOW YOU DIE, IT WILL BE A PEACEFUL AND PAINLESS PROCESS OF LAYING ASIDE NOTHING.

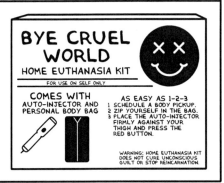

YOU'LL BE DONE USING THE BODY TO PLAY OUT CRAZY, GUILTY IDEAS OF DEATH AND SIN.

LIFE IS A **CLASSROOM** WHERE YOU EITHER CHOOSE THE EGO AS YOUR TEACHER AND LEARN TO STAY ASLEEP, OR YOU CHOOSE THE HOLY SPIRIT AS YOUR TEACHER AND UNLEARN WHAT KEEPS YOU SLEEPING.

THUS, THE PURPOSE OF LIFE IS TO CHOOSE ONCE AGAIN SO THAT YOU CAN UNDO THE ORIGINAL **MISINFORMED CHOICE** THAT LED TO THIS DREAM TO BEGIN WITH -- WHICH, IN TURN, MEANS THAT THE PURPOSE OF THE BODY IS TO RENDER IT UNNECESSARY. [7]

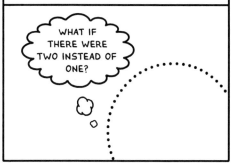

WHAT IF THERE WERE TWO INSTEAD OF ONE?

YOU DON'T HAVE ONE LIFE TO LIVE, EVEN IF THE EGO WOULD LIKE YOU TO BELIEVE YOU DO. YOU HAVE AS MANY LIVES AS IT TAKES YOU TO CHOOSE YOUR RIGHT MIND AND WAKE UP.

THE MEANING OF LIFE IS THAT IT ENDS.

SO, THERE IS NO RUSH. BUT DON'T DELUDE YOURSELF, IF HAPPINESS IS WHAT YOU ARE LOOKING FOR, **NOW** IS ALWAYS THE BEST TIME TO GET TO WAKING UP. WAKING IS WHAT IT IS ALL ABOUT.

THE LAST THING THIS WORLD NEEDS IS MORE DELUSIONAL PEOPLE PLAYING THE EGO'S GO NOWHERE GAMES OF WORLDLY CONQUEST. THOSE GAMES MERELY BREED CONFLICT AND SUSTAIN ILLUSIONS.

I'M KING OF THE MOUNTAIN!

WHAT WILL THINGS LIKE WORLDLY SUCCESS AND PHYSICAL BEAUTY GET YOU IN THIS LIFETIME IF YOU END UP BEING BORN POOR, DEFORMED, AND STARVING IN YOUR NEXT LIFETIME?

NOW, EXCUSE ME. MY LIMO IS WAITING.

ALEX AS BEAUTIFUL SQUIDWARD

YOU CAN'T TRUST THIS DREAM BECAUSE YOU CAN'T TRUST YOUR UNCONSCIOUS GUILT. THAT IS WHY YOU NEED TO GET TO HEALING YOUR GUILT NOW THROUGH TRUE FORGIVENESS.

FORGIVENESS IS THE PURSUIT OF TRUE HAPPINESS BECAUSE IT IS THE PURSUIT OF WAKING UP; IT IS THE PURSUIT OF GOD: THE PURSUIT OF **TRUE** LOVE.

CONVERSELY, THE PURSUIT OF ANYTHING SHORT OF GOD IS THE PURSUIT OF **FAKE** HAPPINESS.

JUST THE MERE ACT OF TAKING A BREATH IS A PURSUIT OF FAKE HAPPINESS. YOU BREATHE BECAUSE **LACK** OF BREATHING IS PAINFUL AND EVENTUALLY LEADS TO BODILY DEATH.

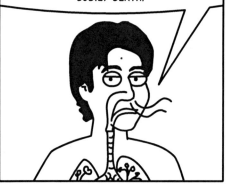

IF YOU COULDN'T BREATHE, YOU'D BE MISERABLE AND THEN DEAD. SO, AS LONG AS YOU ARE ABLE TO BREATHE, YOU ARE HAPPY RELATIVE TO IF YOU COULDN'T BREATHE.

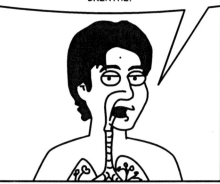

THAT IS THE BASIC DYNAMIC BEHIND ALL OF THE EGO'S FORMS OF SO-CALLED HAPPINESS --

-- THEY ARE PREDICATED ON THE PROMISE OF RELIEF FROM THE MISERABLE, GUILT-LADEN, INSATIABLE SENSE OF LACK STEMMING FROM THE SEEMING SEPARATION FROM GOD --

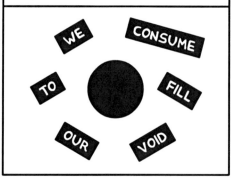

WE CONSUME TO FILL OUR VOID

-- WITHOUT ACTUALLY FIXING IT.

THAT INSATIABLE SENSE OF LACK MANIFESTS AS WHAT WE CALL **APPETITES**. APPETITES STEM FROM THE **FEAR** OF DEATH: OBLIVION.

APPETITES ARE **GETTING** MECHANISMS, REPRESENTING THE EGO'S NEED TO CONFIRM ITSELF. AND THAT IS AS TRUE OF BODY APPETITES AS IT IS OF THE SO-CALLED **HIGHER EGO NEEDS**, LIKE APPROVAL AND RECOGNITION. [8]

BODY APPETITES ARE NOT PHYSICAL IN ORIGIN. THE EGO REGARDS THE BODY AS ITS HOME, AND TRIES TO SATISFY ITSELF THROUGH THE BODY. [8]

KEEP FOCUSED ON THE EXTERNAL WORLD FOR FULFILLMENT. DON'T LOOK WITHIN.

BUT THE IDEA THAT SUCH A THING IS POSSIBLE IS A DECISION OF THE MIND, WHICH HAS BECOME COMPLETELY CONFUSED ABOUT WHAT IS REALLY POSSIBLE. [8]

YOU CAN BE SATISFIED BY PURSUING A LITTLE BIT OF NOTHING AT THE COST OF EVERYTHING.

A PRIME EXAMPLE OF A TYPICAL APPETITE IS SEX. SEX IS AN APPETITE THAT ATTEMPTS TO MIMIC THE CREATIVE JOINING OF HEAVENLY ONENESS BY JOINING BODIES.

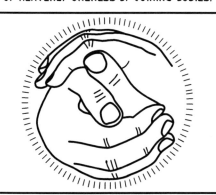

ONLY MINDS ARE JOINED, AND ONLY MINDS CAN TRULY CREATE. BODIES ARE A SEPARATION IDEA AND CANNOT REALLY JOIN OR CREATE. HOWEVER, BODIES CAN COME TOGETHER TO MAKE MORE SEPARATE BODIES.

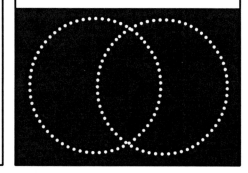

JUST AS EATING, DRINKING, SLEEPING, AND BREATHING ARE USUALLY NECESSARY IN THIS DREAM FOR MAINTAINING BODIES, SEX IS USUALLY NECESSARY FOR MAKING NEW BODIES.

AND FOR AS LONG AS PEOPLE FAIL TO FULLY FORGIVE, THEY WILL REINCARNATE, WHICH WILL REQUIRE NEW BODIES.

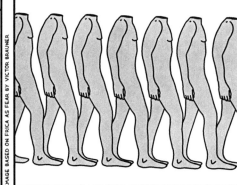

IMAGE BASED ON FRICA AS FEAR BY VICTOR BRAUNER

HOWEVER, THE PROCREATIVE USE OF SEX IS MOST OFTEN AN AFTER EFFECT. MOST SEXUAL ACTIVITY IS PURSUED LIKE AN ADDICTIVE DRUG -- AS AN END IN ITSELF INSTEAD OF A MEANS TO A MEANS.

WHAT PEOPLE ATTEMPT TO ACHIEVE THROUGH SEXUALITY IS AN UPSIDE-DOWN VERSION OF WHAT THEY REALLY WANT BUT ARE AFRAID OF DUE TO THEIR GUILT, WHICH IS TO RETURN TO GOD AS ONE WHOLE MIND.

GOD, WHO IS BEYOND DIFFERENCES AND BINARIES, LIKE MALE AND FEMALE, IS WHO WE ARE REALLY ATTRACTED TO.

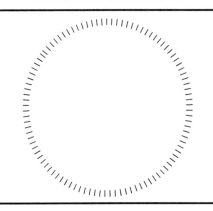

WE REALLY WANT THE ECSTATIC STATE OF CREATIVE ONENESS WITH GOD, NOT A FLEETING ENCOUNTER WITH AN **OBJECT**.

BUT AS A SUBSTITUTE, WE MAKE-UP A FANTASY WORLD IN OUR MINDS AND ASSIGN IMAGINARY POWERS TO BODIES IN AN ATTEMPT TO DERIVE PLEASURE FROM FALSE ASSOCIATIONS. [9]

NOT DEAD ONES

SEXUAL APPETITE IS THUS ALL A MIND GAME THAT HIJACKS THE REPRODUCTIVE MECHANISM TO ASSIGN A CONTRIVED VALUE TO SPECIAL BODIES, BODY PARTS, BODY TYPES, CIRCUMSTANCES, AND SO ON.

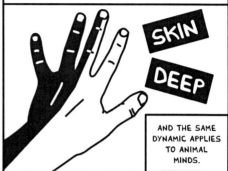

AND THE SAME DYNAMIC APPLIES TO ANIMAL MINDS.

PEOPLE DON'T HAVE SEX WITH PEOPLE, THEY HAVE SEX WITH IDEAS. WHICH IS WHY PEOPLE CAN DEVELOP ALTERNATE SEXUAL ORIENTATIONS AND HAVE ALL VARIETIES OF CHANGEABLE TASTES.

AND THAT IS ALSO WHY PEOPLE CAN BECOME SEXUALLY AROUSED BY DAY DREAMS AND NIGHT DREAMS AND WAKE UP WITH PHYSICAL RESULTS.

THE FACT IS THAT UNLESS SOMEONE GETS PREGNANT, ALL SEX IS ESSENTIALLY JUST MENTAL SELF-GRATIFICATION, REGARDLESS OF HOW MANY FLESH AND BLOOD BODIES ARE INVOLVED.

THE SEEMINGLY EXTERNAL STIMULI IS ALL A PLACEBO GIVEN SEEMING POWER THROUGH ARBITRARY BELIEF.

WE ARE

SEDUCED BY IDEAS

IF YOU WANT TO MAKE TRUE LOVE, YOU WANT TO BE A TRUE FORGIVER. TRUE FORGIVENESS IS THE RIGHT-SIDE-UP FORM OF JOINING IN THIS DREAM.

LACK OF TRUE FORGIVENESS IS A LACK OF TRUE JOINING, WHICH BUILDS TENSION. AND THAT TENSION MANIFESTS AS APPETITES LIKE SEXUAL LIBIDO.

1-900-FORGIVE **HOTLINE**

HEY BABY, I DON'T WANT YOUR BODY SO BAD, BECAUSE I'VE BEEN TRULY FORGIVING.

THE DESIRE TO JOIN

THE BELIEF IN DUALITY

THEREFORE, SEXUAL APPETITE IS A DISTORTION OF THE IMPULSE TO JOIN THROUGH FORGIVENESS. THUS, RATHER THAN ELIMINATE GUILT, IT SUSTAINS GUILT.

AND GUILT NECESSARILY TIES SEX TO THE UNHOLY REALM OF **SPECIAL RELATIONSHIPS**.

HEY, DO YOU WANT TO BE MY GOD SUBSTITUTE FOR AWHILE?

I DON'T KNOW. I'VE BEEN CULTURALLY PROGRAMMED TO PREFER BLACK GOD SUBSTITUTES.

SINCE BODIES ARE THE SUPPOSED HIDING PLACE FROM GUILT IN THE MIND --

-- GUILT COMPELS PEOPLE TO REGARD THEMSELVES AND OTHERS AS BODIES.

THAT KIND OF IDENTIFICATION WITH THE BODY IS THE TRUE MEANING OF THE WORD **TEMPTATION**.

TEMPTATION IS THE EGO'S GAME OF KEEPING PEOPLE ENDLESSLY SEARCHING THROUGH THE BODY BUT NEVER REALLY FINDING -- FOREVER LOCKED IN A FEARFUL LOOP OF INSATIABILITY.

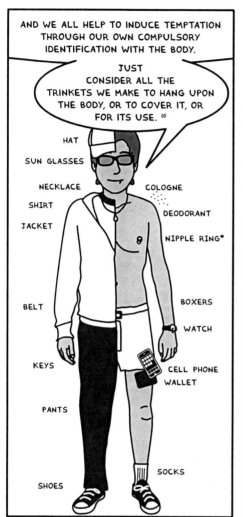

AND WE ALL HELP TO INDUCE TEMPTATION THROUGH OUR OWN COMPULSORY IDENTIFICATION WITH THE BODY.

JUST CONSIDER ALL THE TRINKETS WE MAKE TO HANG UPON THE BODY, OR TO COVER IT, OR FOR ITS USE. [10]

HAT
SUN GLASSES
NECKLACE
COLOGNE
SHIRT
DEODORANT
JACKET
NIPPLE RING*
BELT
BOXERS
WATCH
KEYS
CELL PHONE
WALLET
PANTS
SOCKS
SHOES

* NOT REALLY

CONSIDER ALL THE USELESS THINGS WE MAKE FOR ITS EYES TO SEE. THINK ON THE MANY OFFERINGS WE MAKE FOR ITS PLEASURE. [10]

LOOK. THEY ARE GLOW IN THE DARK AND RIBBED.

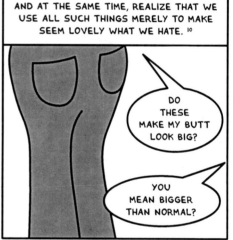

AND AT THE SAME TIME, REALIZE THAT WE USE ALL SUCH THINGS MERELY TO MAKE SEEM LOVELY WHAT WE HATE. [10]

DO THESE MAKE MY BUTT LOOK BIG?

YOU MEAN BIGGER THAN NORMAL?

THE SECRET FACT IS THAT WE MADE OUR BODIES TO SEPARATE AND DIE, AND WE ALL KNOW DAMN WELL THAT NO BODY IS REALLY GOOD ENOUGH.

I WISH I COULD FLY.

I WISH I WAS BULLET PROOF.

I WISH I HAD SUPER SPEED.

I WISH I HAD X-RAY VISION.

137

YET, WE NONETHELESS EMPLOY THESE HATED THINGS TO DRAW EACH OTHER TO OURSELVES, AND TO ATTRACT THE BODY'S EYES. [10]

DID YOU LIKE THE PICTURE I SENT YOU?

WHEN WE DO THAT, WE OFFER EACH OTHER A CROWN OF **THORNS**, NOT RECOGNIZING IT FOR WHAT IT IS. AND WE TRY TO JUSTIFY OUR OWN INTERPRETATION OF THE BODY'S VALUE BY THE OTHER'S ACCEPTANCE. [10]

YET, STILL, THE GIFT PROCLAIMS THE OTHER'S WORTHLESSNESS TO US, AS THE OTHER'S ACCEPTANCE AND DELIGHT ACKNOWLEDGES THE LACK OF VALUE HE OR SHE PLACES ON HIM OR HERSELF. [10]

GIFTS ARE NOT MADE THROUGH BODIES, IF THEY BE TRULY GIVEN AND RECEIVED. FOR BODIES CAN NEITHER OFFER NOR ACCEPT; HOLD OUT NOR TAKE. ONLY THE MIND CAN VALUE, AND ONLY THE MIND DECIDES ON WHAT IT WOULD RECEIVE AND GIVE. [11]

WOO HOO! THIS IS MY BEST BIRTHDAY EVER!

AND EVERY GIFT IT OFFERS DEPENDS ON WHAT IT WANTS. IT WILL ADORN ITS CHOSEN HOME MOST CAREFULLY, MAKING IT READY TO RECEIVE THE **GIFTS** IT WANTS BY OFFERING THEM TO THOSE WHO COME UNTO ITS CHOSEN HOME, OR THOSE IT WOULD ATTRACT TO IT. [10]

TRUTH OR **ILLUSION?**

AND THERE THEY WILL EXCHANGE THEIR GIFTS, OFFERING AND RECEIVING WHAT THEIR MINDS **JUDGE** TO BE WORTHY OF THEM. [10]

MERELY OFFER THE GIFT OF THE BODY AND YOU OFFER A CROWN OF **THORNS** IN AN INSANE GAME OF SACRIFICE. [10]

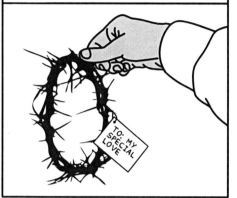

OFFER INSTEAD THE GIFT OF TRUE FORGIVENESS AND YOU ARE SET **FREE** BY IDENTIFYING WITH SPIRIT. [10]

TO GIVE THE GIFT OF TRUE FORGIVENESS IS TO MAKE TRUE LOVE WITH EVERYONE ON THE LEVEL OF MIND; IT IS TO UNDO GUILT AND THUS RESTORE THE UNWAVERING CREATIVE ECSTASY OF HEAVENLY ONENESS. THEREFORE, A TRUE LOVE MAKER IS A TRUE FORGIVER.

IMAGE BASED ON THE KISS BY GUSTAV KLIMT

AND SO, IT SHOULD COME AS NO SURPRISE THAT CELIBACY IS QUITE NATURAL FOR THOSE WHO **TASTE** HEAVEN; TRUE CELIBACY IS OF THE MIND AND **TASTING** HEAVEN PUTS THINGS INTO PERSPECTIVE.

YET, WE ALL HAVE TO START FROM WHERE WE THINK WE ARE. WE CAN'T AND WON'T GIVE UP ANYTHING WE SEE AS REAL. AND WHATEVER WE BELIEVE IN IS REAL TO US.

I BELIEVE THAT I AM ALONE UNLESS ANOTHER BODY IS WITH ME.

TRYING TO PLAY PRETEND ENLIGHTENMENT BY MODIFYING BEHAVIOR INSTEAD OF THE MIND DOESN'T WORK; IT JUST BREEDS **CONFLICT** AND MAKES THE BODY OUT TO BE REAL.

THAT IS THE PROBLEM WITH THE REPRESSIVE ATTITUDES TOWARD SEX FOUND IN MANY **RELIGIONS** AND OTHER SOCIAL INSTITUTIONS.

HOW ABOUT FOR PENANCE YOU AND I GO GET A DRINK?

AND THAT IS ALSO THE PROBLEM WITH EXTRA-PERMISSIVE ATTITUDES TOWARD SEX THAT **GLORIFY** IT AND TREAT IT AS IF IT IS A MEANS TO ENLIGHTENMENT OR SOMETHING.

ALL SUCH ATTITUDES ARE THE SAME IN THAT THEY IMPLICITLY MAKE THE BODY REAL AND THUS THE MIND MINDLESS.

GUILT IN THE MIND IS WHAT BINDS US TO THE BODY AND COERCES OUR BELIEF IN IT, WHICH IS WHAT MAKES IT SEEMINGLY REAL. THEREFORE, FORGIVENESS IS WHAT WILL SET US FREE.

WHAT WE NEED TO FORGIVE IS ALMOST ALWAYS TRACEABLE TO A BELIEF IN THE BODY IN SOME WAY.

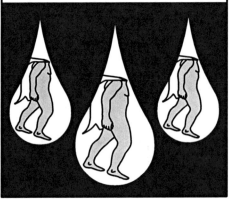

THIS DREAM IS NOTHING AND THE BODY IS NOTHING. TO WAKE UP WE ARE ASKED TO GIVE UP NOTHING. BUT ONLY WHEN WE TRULY REALIZE THAT NOTHING IS NOTHING WILL WE GIVE IT UP. SO, AS LONG AS NOTHING IS SOMETHING TO YOU, DON'T DENY THAT FACT. THAT IS PART OF YOUR FORGIVENESS.

I HAVE OFTEN WALKED DOWN THIS STREET BEFORE; BUT THE FLOWERS NEVER EVER SMELLED SO SWEET BEFORE. ALL AT ONCE AM I OUT OF MY MIND. KNOWING I'M ON THE STREET WHERE HER BODY LIVES.

ALEX AS FREDDY EYNSFORD-HILL; MY FAIR LADY

THE HOLY SPIRIT DOES NOT DEMAND YOU SACRIFICE THE HOPE OF THE BODY'S PLEASURE; THE HOLY SPIRIT KNOWS THE BODY HAS NO HOPE OF PLEASURE. [II] THE BODY DOESN'T **FEEL**, ONLY THE MIND DOES.

YOU JUST HAVE TO REMEMBER YOUR SPIRITUAL SELF AND INCLUDE THE HOLY SPIRIT IN EVERYTHING YOU DO. THAT WAY YOU'LL USE EVERYTHING YOU DO FOR FORGIVENESS.

BUT WAIT! WHAT A WONDERFUL FEELING WHEN I REMEMBER THAT SHE IS REALLY IN MY MIND.

THE HOLY SPIRIT CASTS NO JUDGMENT ON DREAMS EXCEPT TO POINT OUT THAT THEY AREN'T TRUE. SO, YOU HAVE NOTHING TO HIDE.

THE CASE YOU BUILT AGAINST YOURSELF AND YOUR BROTHERS IS DISMISSED. DREAMS AREN'T REAL.

AS YOU PRACTICE TRUE FORGIVENESS, IT WILL BE LIKE A REVERSE DRUG ADDICTION.

141

142

MOST THINGS PEOPLE DO, THEY DO PRECISELY BECAUSE OF GUILT. IF THEY DID EVERYTHING THEY DO WITHOUT GUILT, THEY WOULDN'T DO MANY OF THE THINGS THEY DO.

AFTER ALL, WHO HAS NEED TO GET **DRUNK**, OR ACCUMULATE **WEALTH**, OR EVEN **BREATHE** UNLESS GUILT IN THE MIND COMPELS A SEARCH FOR HAPPINESS THROUGH PETTY, TRANSIENT MANIPULATIONS OF A **MORTAL** BODY?

THE FACT IS THAT A HEALED, GUILTLESS MIND OFTEN DOESN'T STICK AROUND IN THE BODY FOR VERY LONG AFTER IT HAS AWAKENED.

FORGIVE YOU GUYS, I'M GOING HOME.

AND THERE IS A REASON FOR THAT. A HEALED, GUILTLESS MIND HAS SOMETHING INCOMPARABLY BETTER THAN ANYTHING THIS DREAM OF BODIES HAS TO OFFER.

BUT GETTING TO THAT POINT TAKES PERSISTENT FORGIVENESS; IT TAKES USING ALL YOUR RELATIONSHIPS, INTERESTS, AND PROBLEMS IN THIS DREAM AS OPPORTUNITIES TO PRACTICE FORGIVENESS.

TO THE HOLY SPIRIT, THE BODY IS SOLELY A **COMMUNICATION** TOOL FOR JOINING MINDS THROUGH FORGIVENESS, WHICH TEACHES PEOPLE THAT THEY ARE NOT BODIES.

IN THE INTERIM, THAT DOESN'T PRECLUDE THE FEEBLE PURSUITS OF THE BODY, BUT IN THE END IT DOES TRANSCEND THEM.

THE LOVING CALL FROM GOD TO FORGIVE AND RETURN TO ONENESS IS DISTORTED BY THE EGO'S PRISM OF GUILT.

PRISM OF GUILT

HUNGRY HUNGRY HUNGRY HUNGRY HUNGRY HUNGRY HUNGRY HUNG
LUSTFUL LUSTFUL LUSTFUL LUSTFUL LUSTFUL LUSTFUL LUST
HOT HOT HOT HOT HOT HOT HOT HOT HOT HOT HOT HOT
TIRED TIRED TIRED TIRED TIRED TIRED TIRED TIRED T
THIRSTY THIRSTY THIRSTY THIRSTY THIRSTY THIRSTY THI
POOR POOR POOR POOR POOR POOR POOR POOR POOP
RESTLESS RESTLESS RESTLESS RESTLESS RESTLESS RESTLES
IGNORED IGNORED IGNORED IGNORED IGNOR
COLD COLD COLD COLD COLD COLD COLD COLD COLD CO

THE FEEBLE PURSUITS OF THE BODY ARE THE EGO'S DECEPTIVE WAY OF TURNING THE IMPULSE TO JOIN AND FORGIVE INTO SOMETHING PHYSICAL AND FLEETING.

NOTHING SHORT OF EVERYTHING WILL EVER REALLY SATISFY YOU.

YET, THIS DREAM IS CERTAINLY NOTHING TO SCORN. ANY GUILT AND UNPLEASANTNESS YOU SEE IS NOT OUT THERE IN THE ILLUSION, IT IS IN YOUR MIND. FORGIVE IT.

LCD   PHONY

SEEN AS IT REALLY IS, THROUGH THE EYES OF FORGIVENESS, THIS WORLD IS A PLACE OF LOVELY MIRACLE WORKING.

SO, TURN TO YOUR GUIDE, THE HOLY SPIRIT, AND GET MIRACLE WORKING.

ILLUMINATE THIS IMAGE WITH BRIGHT LIGHT AND STARE AT THE CENTER DOT FOR AT LEAST 20 SECONDS. THEN LOOK AT A BLANK WALL AND BLINK REPEATEDLY.

144

WE ARE ALL CONSTANTLY IN A STATE OF PRAYER, BUT TO GET TO THE STATE OF TRUE PRAYER REQUIRES CLIMBING THE LADDER OF PRAYER.

THE MOST BASIC FORM OF PRAYER IS MERELY WANTING OUT OF A SENSE OF SCARCITY AND LACK. [2]

WANTING DOESN'T REQUIRE MAKING AN APPEAL TO GOD, NOR DOES IT EVEN REQUIRE A BELIEF IN GOD. IT IS ESSENTIALLY THE BASE STATE OF THE SPLIT MIND UNDER THE CONTROL OF THE EGO.

THUS, THE LOWEST FORM OF PRAYER LOOKS MERELY TO THE UNIVERSE FOR FULFILLMENT.

GUILT

FOR EXAMPLE, PEOPLE ANSWER THEIR PRAYERS FOR THINGS LIKE MORE MONEY BY DOING THINGS LIKE GOING TO A JOB FOR 8 HOURS A DAY AND WORKING.

NEXT STOP, WILLOUGHBY!

PLEASE KILL ME.

PEOPLE ANSWER THEIR PRAYERS FOR MORE AIR BY TAKING BREATHS.

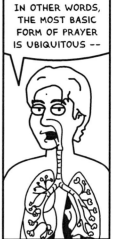

IN OTHER WORDS, THE MOST BASIC FORM OF PRAYER IS UBIQUITOUS --

146

-- IT IS THE FORM OF PRAYER OF LOBSTERS AND CELLS AND ATOMS.

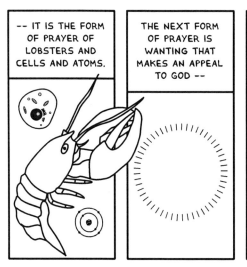

THE NEXT FORM OF PRAYER IS WANTING THAT MAKES AN APPEAL TO GOD --

-- IT IS THE FORM OF PRAYER THAT IS TRADITIONALLY ACCEPTED AS PRAYER; IT IS PRAYER TO GOD WITHOUT UNDERSTANDING.

DEAR GOD, YOU CONTROL THE WORLD, SO GIVE ME WHAT I WANT.

PRAYING TO GOD FOR THINGS IN THIS DREAM MAKES NO SENSE TO ANYONE WHO UNDERSTANDS THAT THIS UNIVERSE IS INDEED A DREAM. GOD HAS NOTHING TO DO WITH THIS DREAM BECAUSE FORTUNATELY, GOD IS NOT INSANE.

THUS, IT SHOULD COME AS NO SURPRISE THAT EVERYONE WHO EVER TRIED TO USE PRAYER TO ASK FOR SOMETHING HAS EXPERIENCED WHAT APPEARED TO BE FAILURE. [3]

DAMN, MY INSPIRED LOTTERY NUMBERS WERE A SHAM!

THE LOTTERY JUNE 27

3 8 16 22 40 50

THAT IS BECAUSE IT IS NOT SOME 'THING' THAT WE REALLY WANT AND NEED. WHAT WE REALLY WANT AND NEED IS GOD, BUT OUR GUILT KEEPS US SEEKING ONLY SUBSTITUTES.

YOU WANT A LITTLE BIT OF SPECIAL NOTHINGNESS, NOT TOTAL ONENESS.

IN THAT SENSE, FROM WITHIN THIS DREAM, THE ONLY MEANINGFUL PRAYER IS FOR FORGIVENESS. FORGIVENESS IS PRAYER'S ALLY. [4]

DEAR GOD, HELP ME GET RID OF MY UNCONSCIOUS FEAR OF YOU.

FORGIVENESS IS SOMETHING WE DO WITH THE HOLY SPIRIT BY JOINING WITH THE HOLY SPIRIT IN PRAYER TO LOOK AT OUR PROJECTIONS.

DEAR HOLY SPIRIT, LET ME FORGIVE MY UNCONSCIOUS FEAR WHEN I SEE IT IN MY PROJECTED WORLD.

HOWEVER, WE WON'T EVER REALLY JOIN WITH THE HOLY SPIRIT UNTIL WE FIRST FORGIVE THE HOLY SPIRIT -- AND THAT INCLUDES ANY SYMBOLS EQUIVALENT TO THE HOLY SPIRIT, ESPECIALLY **JESUS.**

THE HOLY SPIRIT DOESN'T NEED OUR FORGIVENESS, BUT WE NEED OUR FORGIVENESS.

FORGIVING THE HOLY SPIRIT STARTS WITH RECOGNIZING THAT THE HOLY SPIRIT IS NOT SOMEONE SEPARATE FROM US BUT IS IN FACT THE **TRUE US** THAT WE FORGOT ABOUT WHEN WE PRETENDED TO BE THE EGO.

SPLIT 2
RIGHT AND WRONG MIND

REMEMBER, IT IS IMPOSSIBLE TO LOVE SOMEONE WHOM YOU PERCEIVE AS DIFFERENT FROM YOURSELF. BECAUSE IF SOMEONE IS DIFFERENT FROM YOU, THEN THAT PERSON HAS SOMETHING YOU DON'T HAVE.

I LOVE YOU AS LONG AS I BELIEVE YOU ARE THE MISSING PIECE THAT CAN FILL THE IMAGINARY VOID IN MY HEART.

THAT IS THE DYNAMIC BEHIND **SPECIAL RELATIONSHIPS;** THEY ARE ABOUT STEALING FROM OTHERS WHAT WE UNCONSCIOUSLY BELIEVE THEY **STOLE** FROM US.

SO, IF WE WANT TO WAKE UP, WE **DON'T** WANT A SPECIAL RELATIONSHIP WITH THE HOLY SPIRIT, WE WANT A **HOLY** RELATIONSHIP.

A HOLY RELATIONSHIP IS PREDICATED ON **SPIRIT**, **EQUALITY**, AND **ONENESS**. AN UNHOLY, SPECIAL RELATIONSHIP IS PREDICATED ON BODIES, DIFFERENCES, AND INCOMPLETENESS.

IF YOUR RELATIONSHIP WITH THE HOLY SPIRIT ISN'T HOLY, IT WILL BE SPECIAL, AND YOU'LL INEVITABLY USE IT FOR GUILT PROJECTION WHEN YOUR SPECIAL NEEDS AREN'T MET AS YOU THINK THEY SHOULD BE.

OH GOD, WHY HAVE YOU FORSAKEN ME?

THE WHOLE POINT OF LEARNING TO JOIN WITH THE HOLY SPIRIT IS TO GET BACK WHAT YOU REALLY WANT.

BRING ILLUSIONS TO THE TRUTH, NOT TRUTH TO ILLUSIONS.

AND WHAT YOU REALLY WANT, BUT ARE TERRIFIED OF, IS THE COMPLETE LOVE OF ONENESS WITH GOD -- NOT THE SHABBY EGO SUBSTITUTES FOR GOD THAT PEOPLE FRUITLESSLY SEEK IN THIS DREAM.

I WANT TO BE SPECIAL. I WANT ILLUSIONS.

DON'T CARE HOW, I WANT IT NOW.

GOOD BAD

REFERENCE TO WILLY WONKA & THE CHOCOLATE FACTORY

GUILTY, UNCONSCIOUS FEAR OF GOD IS WHY PEOPLE PRAY FOR THINGS LIKE 100 MILLION DOLLARS. PEOPLE BELIEVE THAT IF THEY HAD 100 MILLION DOLLARS THEY'D HAVE ACCESS TO ENOUGH RESOURCES TO BUILD THEIR OWN SUBSTITUTE HEAVEN.

DEAR GOD, IF ONLY I HAD MILLIONS OF DOLLARS ALL MY UNCONSCIOUS GUILT WOULD BE GONE.

BUT HEAVEN CANNOT BE SUBSTITUTED. MONEY CAN'T BUY GUILTLESSNESS, ONLY TRUE FORGIVENESS CAN.

NO MATTER WHAT KIND OF SEEMINGLY FAIRY TALE LIFE OF MATERIAL ABUNDANCE YOU MIGHT MANAGE TO FIND IN THIS DREAM --

-- IT WON'T CHANGE THE INNER CONTENT OF YOUR MIND, NOR WILL IT LAST. AFTER ALL, MATERIAL ABUNDANCE OPERATES UNDER THE RULES OF THE EGO WHEREBY ONE MUST LOSE FOR ANOTHER TO GAIN, INEVITABLY SUSTAINING GUILT. JUST THINK, IF EVERYONE HAD 10 MILLION DOLLARS, 10 MILLION DOLLARS WOULDN'T BE WORTH MUCH ANYMORE.

ALEX AS RICHIE RICH; RICHIE RICH © HARVEY ENTERTAINMENT

MATERIAL ABUNDANCE HAS NO CORRELATION TO SPIRITUAL ABUNDANCE; IT IS NO MORE OR LESS SPIRITUAL TO BE RICH THAN IT IS TO BE POOR.

THE SCRIPT OF THIS DREAM IS WRITTEN. THE ONLY QUESTION IS: DO YOU WANT THE EGO'S **ELONGATED** SCRIPT OR THE HOLY SPIRIT'S **SHORTENED** SCRIPT?

150

IF SOMETHING LIKE OBTAINING 100 MILLION DOLLARS DOESN'T COMPLY WITH ANY VARIATIONS OF THIS DREAM'S SCRIPT, IT WON'T HAPPEN BECAUSE IT WON'T BE IN THE SCRIPT.

PRAYING FOR THINGS THAT ARE ACTUALLY IN THE SCRIPT IS HOW ANSWERS TO PRAYERS SEEMINGLY MANIFEST IN THIS DREAM.

WE ARE ALL TECHNICALLY PSYCHIC. WE ALREADY WROTE THE SCRIPT OF THIS UNIVERSE AFTER ALL.

HOWEVER, MOST OF US KEEP OUR PSYCHIC ABILITIES **UNCONSCIOUS**. THE EGO LOVES SURPRISES -- ESPECIALLY UNPLEASANT ONES, SINCE THEY REMIND US OF THE SEEMING SPLIT FROM GOD.

AHHHH! HUGE ICEBERG DEAD AHEAD!

PSYCHIC INFORMATION CAN ONLY ENTER THE SCRIPT IF IT IS SCRIPTED TO DO SO. THAT IS WHY PEOPLE WHO MAY HAVE SOME CONSCIOUS PSYCHIC ABILITIES NONETHELESS CAN'T NECESSARILY PREDICT LOTTERY NUMBERS; THAT INFORMATION ISN'T AVAILABLE TO THEM IN THE SCRIPT.

THE HOLY SPIRIT WORKS WITH YOU ON THE **MIND** LEVEL, NOT THE PHYSICAL LEVEL.

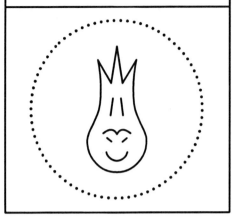

SO, IF YOU ASK AND SEEMINGLY RECEIVE, IT DOESN'T REALLY MEAN ANYTHING. THE FACT IS THAT MOST WISHES ARE FOR SPECIAL LOVE RELATIONSHIPS OF VARIOUS FORMS. AND SPECIAL LOVE RELATIONSHIPS ARE THE EGO'S **MOST BOASTED GIFT.** [10]

THIS SPECIAL THING WILL GIVE YOU THE SPECIALNESS THAT GOD WON'T.

GOD IS YOUR SOURCE. IF YOU LOOK TO THINGS IN THIS DREAM WORLD AS YOUR SOURCE, YOU SET YOURSELF UP FOR SCARCITY AND FAILURE.

MY FAMILY, MY POSSESSIONS, AND MY LUCRATIVE CAREER ARE MY SOURCE.

ANYTHING IN THIS WORLD THAT YOU BELIEVE IS GOOD AND VALUABLE AND WORTH STRIVING FOR CAN HURT YOU, AND WILL DO SO. [6]

NY TIMES BESTSELLER

YOUR IMMORTAL
REALTY

$

RETIRE RICH WITH
REAL ESTATE

BY THE REALTORS ASSOCIATION

NOT BECAUSE IT HAS THE POWER TO HURT, BUT JUST BECAUSE YOU HAVE DENIED IT IS BUT AN ILLUSION, AND MADE IT REAL. [6]

BY TURNING TO YOUR TRUE SOURCE (**GOD**) INSTEAD OF ILLUSORY SOURCES (**WORLDLY IDOLS**) YOU WILL TAP INTO THE LOVE THAT WILL ALLOW YOU TO FOLLOW VARIATIONS OF THE SCRIPT THAT ARE MOST CONDUCIVE TO YOU RETURNING HOME.

I HAVE ONLY WHAT I GIVE. TO HAVE PEACE I GIVE PEACE. I GIVE UNTO OTHERS ONLY THE GIFTS I WANT TO ACCEPT FOR MYSELF.

AND THE MOST CONDUCIVE SCRIPT TO YOU RETURNING HOME IS OFTEN ONE WHERE THINGS WORK OUT GENERALLY FINE, YOUR FORGIVENESS LESSONS ARE RELATIVELY GENTLE, AND YOUR PHYSICAL NEEDS ARE MET SUFFICIENTLY FOR YOU TO SEEK GOD FOR FULFILLMENT INSTEAD OF ILLUSIONS.

IN THEATERS THIS SUMMER

THE GENTLE AWAKENING

IF YOU SEEK FIRST THE KINGDOM OF HEAVEN, ALL ELSE WILL BE GIVEN TO YOU FOR YOU TO ACTUALLY WAKE UP AND RETURN TO YOUR TRUE HOME.

THEREFORE, THE SECRET OF TRUE PRAYER IS TO FORGET THE THINGS YOU THINK YOU NEED. TO ASK FOR THE SPECIFIC IS MUCH THE SAME AS TO LOOK ON SIN AND THEN FORGIVE IT.

YOU ARE REAL. BUT I WON'T PUNISH YOU FOR NOW.

MAKING SIN REAL IS FALSE FORGIVENESS, AND MAKING SPECIFIC WANTS REAL IS FALSE PRAYER.

THE SPECIFIC THINGS YOU THINK YOU WANT AND NEED ARE A PRODUCT OF YOUR UNCONSCIOUS GUILT AND THUS, IN THE BIG PICTURE, RECEIVING THEM OFTEN ISN'T IN YOUR BEST INTEREST.

DEAR GOD, I WANT ILLUSIONS -- I WANT THE PAST REPEATED.

IF YOU ARE PRACTICING FORGIVENESS WITH THE HOLY SPIRIT, YOU WILL BE DISSOLVING YOUR GUILT. AND IT IS YOUR GUILT THAT MAKES YOU FEEL LACKING, FEARFULLY ASKING FOR SUBSTITUTES FOR HEAVEN TO DROWN OUT THE FOUL STENCH OF DEATH THAT PERMEATES THIS DREAM.

THIS UNIVERSE IS A TURD; IT IS THE EXCREMENT OF OUR PERCEIVED CANNIBALISTIC CONSUMPTION OF GOD. DON'T WASTE YOUR TIME TRYING TO POLISH A TURD; YOUR RESULTS WILL AT BEST ONLY BE TEMPORARY AND WILL NEVER COMPLETELY SATISFY YOU.

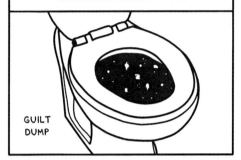

GUILT DUMP

IF YOU WANT TO PRAY TRULY, START BY PUTTING THE HOLY SPIRIT IN CHARGE OF EVERYTHING YOU DO. WHICH IS TO SAY, YOU SHOULD PUT YOUR RIGHT MIND IN CHARGE OF EVERYTHING YOU DO.

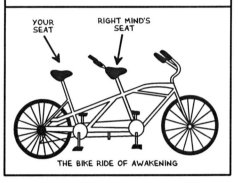

YOUR SEAT

RIGHT MIND'S SEAT

THE BIKE RIDE OF AWAKENING

EVERY MORNING, IT WOULD BE A GOOD IDEA TO STOP FOR A MOMENT AND SAY: HOLY SPIRIT, I PUT YOU IN CHARGE OF EVERYTHING I DO TODAY.

I'VE ALWAYS WANTED TO HAVE A BOSS JUST LIKE YOU.

WON'T YOU BE MY MENTOR?

ALEX AS MISTER ROGERS

YOU ARE ASSURED A HAPPY DAY EVERYDAY AS LONG AS YOU ARE WILLING TO MAKE **ALL** DECISIONS WITH THE HOLY SPIRIT.ª THE FACT IS THAT YOU CANNOT MAKE DECISIONS BY YOURSELF ANYWAY.ª

YOU ALWAYS EITHER MAKE DECISIONS WITH THE EGO OR WITH THE HOLY SPIRIT. AND IF YOU ARE UNSURE WITH WHOM YOU ARE MAKING YOUR DECISIONS SIMPLY ASK YOURSELF, "HOW DO I FEEL RIGHT NOW?"

WITH THE HOLY SPIRIT IN CHARGE, YOU'LL CEASE TO JUDGE. BECAUSE JUDGMENT IS THE EGO'S GAME. YOU'LL FORGIVE INSTEAD.

PEACE VS. GUILT

THE ONLY VALID JUDGMENT IS BETWEEN TRUTH AND ILLUSIONS. TRYING TO SORT ILLUSIONS INTO GOOD AND BAD IS WHY EVERYDAY ISN'T A HAPPY DAY.

HIERARCHIES OF ILLUSIONS
COMMON JUDGMENTS

RAINY DAY = BAD
SUNNY DAY = GOOD
LOSING MONEY = BAD
GETTING MONEY = GOOD
CALLS FOR LOVE = BAD
EXPRESSIONS OF LOVE = GOOD
SAMENESS = BAD
SPECIALNESS = GOOD

PUTTING THE HOLY SPIRIT IN CHARGE MEANS PUTTING GOD BACK IN CHARGE, WHICH EXTINGUISHES THE INHERENT GUILT THAT COMES WITH EGO-DEPENDENT SELF-RELIANCE.

AND TO ACCENTUATE HANDING YOUR DAYS OVER TO THE HOLY SPIRIT, IT WOULD ALSO BE WISE TO TAKE A FEW MINUTES TO MEDITATE DAILY AND JOIN WITH YOUR SOURCE, GOD, WITH EYES CLOSED IN A QUIET MEDITATIVE SONG OF PRAYER.

IMAGINE GOD AS A PERFECT, FLAWLESS, ALL-ENCOMPASSING LIGHT AND BASK IN THE LIGHT'S PURE, COMFORTING LOVE.

WHILE DOING THAT, THINK OF ALL THE THINGS YOU THINK YOU WANT AND NEED IN THIS DREAM, INCLUDING THINGS YOU THINK YOU LOST, LIKE SPECIAL LOVED ONES WHO HAVE SEEMINGLY DIED OR GONE.

THEN LET ALL THOSE THINGS DISSOLVE INTO THE LIGHT OF GOD AS IF TO SAY:

GOD, EVERYTHING I WANT IS IN THE UNDIVIDED TOTALITY OF YOU, I WILL NOT ASK FOR A LITTLE BIT OF NOTHING WHEN IT IS ONLY EVERYTHING THAT CAN TRULY SATISFY.

IF YOU PRACTICE PRAYING LIKE THAT DAILY AND TRULY MEAN IT, THE ECHO OF THAT SONG OF PRAYER WILL COME BACK TO YOU IN THE FORM OF INSPIRATION FROM THE HOLY SPIRIT WHENEVER A PATH IS AVAILABLE IN THE SCRIPT THAT WILL HELP YOU BE A HAPPY LEARNER.

THAT IS **THE SECRET** THAT HELPS YOU RETURN HOME -- AS OPPOSED TO THE SECRET THAT SIMPLY HELPS YOU POLISH TURDS.

ALL WANT COMES FROM THE BELIEF IN SEPARATION FROM GOD. THEREFORE, THE SATISFACTION OF ALL WANT IS THE REMOVAL OF ALL THE BARRIERS SET UP TO BLOCK THE LOVE OF ONENESS.

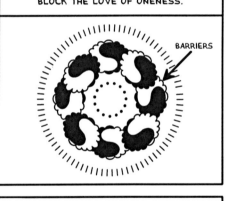

BARRIERS

WHETHER YOU ARE HUNGRY, LUSTFUL, COLD, BROKE, TIRED, WHATEVER, ALL OF IT IS A SENSE OF LACK THAT ONLY GOD CAN TRULY SATISFY, NOT ILLUSIONS.

THUS, THE GNOSIS OF TRUE PRAYER IS THIS:

PUT THE HOLY SPIRIT IN CHARGE OF EVERY DAY.

SEEK ONENESS (GOD) FIRST INSTEAD OF SUBSTITUTES FOR ONENESS.

AND, MOST IMPORTANTLY, TRULY FORGIVE.

PRACTICE MAKES PERFECT. IF YOU CAN LEARN TO DO THOSE THREE THINGS, YOU'LL BE CHANGING YOUR MIND ABOUT THIS DREAM INSTEAD OF POINTLESSLY TRYING TO CHANGE THIS DREAM.

AND THAT IS YOUR TICKET HOME.

YET, EVEN THOUGH WE'VE ALL ALREADY AWAKENED OUTSIDE OF TIME, FROM OUR PERSPECTIVE, Y'SHUA IS STILL HERE WITH US IN OUR MINDS JUST AS WE ARE ALL SEEMINGLY STILL HERE WITH US IN OUR MINDS AS ONE HOLY SPIRIT.

IN 1965, **DR. WILLIAM THETFORD**, THE DIRECTOR OF CLINICAL PSYCHOLOGY AT THE COLUMBIA-PRESBYTERIAN HOSPITAL IN NEW YORK, UNEXPECTEDLY ANNOUNCED TO A COLLEAGUE OF HIS, A RESEARCH PSYCHOLOGIST NAMED **DR. HELEN SCHUCMAN**, THAT HE WAS FED UP WITH THE COMPETITION, AGGRESSION, AND ANGER THAT PERMEATED THEIR PROFESSIONAL LIVES AND EXTENDED INTO THEIR ATTITUDES AND RELATIONSHIPS. THETFORD CONCLUDED THAT THERE MUST BE ANOTHER WAY OF LIVING -- IN HARMONY RATHER THAN DISCORD -- AND HE WAS DETERMINED TO FIND IT. TO THEIR MUTUAL AMAZEMENT, HELEN ENTHUSIASTICALLY VOLUNTEERED TO JOIN HIM IN A COLLABORATIVE SEARCH.

158

SOON THEREAFTER, HELEN SCHUCMAN BEGAN TO EXPERIENCE AN **INNER VOICE** THAT IDENTIFIED ITSELF AS THE HISTORICAL **JESUS**.

THIS IS A COURSE IN MIRACLES. PLEASE TAKE NOTES.

OVER THE COURSE OF SEVERAL YEARS, HELEN, WITH HELP FROM WILLIAM THETFORD, RECORDED, IN WRITING, THE WORDS OF THE INNER VOICE TO FORM SOMETHING CALLED **A COURSE IN MIRACLES**.

A COURSE IN MIRACLES IS A 1200-PAGE SELF-STUDY COURSE ON HOW TO THINK WITH THE HOLY SPIRIT AND, IN THE END, REAWAKEN TO GOD; IT IS ESSENTIALLY THE BOOK Y'SHUA NEVER GOT A CHANCE TO WRITE IN HIS OWN TIME.

THERE ARE, OF COURSE, MANY DOCUMENTS THAT CLAIM TO HAVE BEEN CHANNELED FROM JESUS.

THERE ARE EVEN DOCUMENTS THAT CLAIM TO HAVE BEEN CHANNELED FROM GOD. NOT THE LEAST OF WHICH IS THE BIBLE.

HOWEVER, THEY CAN'T ALL BE RIGHT. ESPECIALLY SINCE THEY OFTEN CONTRADICT EACH OTHER AND DEMONSTRATE A LEVEL OF SPIRITUAL UNDERSTANDING THAT IS AT BEST MEDIOCRE AND OFTEN DOWNRIGHT LAME.

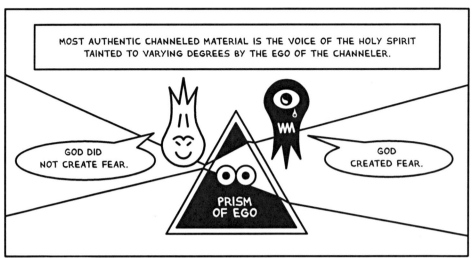

MOST AUTHENTIC CHANNELED MATERIAL IS THE VOICE OF THE HOLY SPIRIT TAINTED TO VARYING DEGREES BY THE EGO OF THE CHANNELER.

GOD DID NOT CREATE FEAR.

PRISM OF EGO

GOD CREATED FEAR.

UNAUTHENTIC CHANNELED MATERIAL IS EITHER A LIE OR THE UNENLIGHTENED VOICE OF AN UNENLIGHTENED SOUL MAKING CLAIMS TO THE CONTRARY.

THE DEPTH AND CONSISTENCY OF A COURSE IN MIRACLES SPEAKS FOR ITSELF AND PUTS IT IN A CLASS OF ITS OWN.

THIS IS THE CLOSEST THING TO THE REAL DEAL THAT YOU'LL FIND IN THIS DREAM.

SEA OF THE UNCONSCIOUS

FOREST OF SACRIFICE

HOME

IDOL CITY

SWAMP OF DEATH

THE GREAT WALL OF FEAR

Y'SHUA DOESN'T CLAIM THAT THE COURSE IS THE ONLY PATH HOME TO GOD. AFTER ALL, IT IS CALLED **A** COURSE IN MIRACLES, NOT **THE** COURSE IN MIRACLES. HOWEVER, Y'SHUA DOES CLAIM THAT IT IS BY FAR THE **FASTEST** PATH HOME. THAT IS BECAUSE IT DEALS DIRECTLY WITH THE THING THAT KEEPS US DREAMING: OUR GUILT. [1]

PLAINS OF DESPERATION

YOU ARE HERE

SPECIAL RELATIONSHIP MOUNTAINS

FORGIVENESS RIVER

DESERT OF GRIEVANCES

ALL ROADS LEAD TO GOD. THE SCRIPT IS WRITTEN AND THE END OF THE DREAM IS CERTAIN. HOWEVER, MOST ROADS HOME TO GOD CATER TO THE EGO, THUS MAKING THEM LONG AND ARDUOUS.

Y'SHUA WAITED 2000 YEARS TO GIVE A COURSE IN MIRACLES BECAUSE THE **DAWN** OF THE THIRD MILLENNIUM WAS THE FIRST TIME IN HUMAN HISTORY THAT THE COURSE HAD ANY HOPE OF BEING GENERALLY TRANSMISSIBLE AND COMPREHENSIBLE WITHOUT PARALYZING DISTORTIONS.

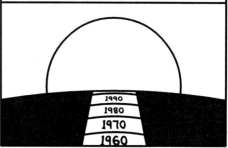

TODAY, MORE PEOPLE ARE LITERATE THAN EVER. THE TRANSMISSION OF INFORMATION IS EASIER THAN EVER, AND HUMANITY'S UNDERSTANDING OF THE MIND AND THE UNIVERSE IS GENERALLY MORE SOPHISTICATED THAN EVER. HOWEVER, JUST AS THE HOLY SPIRIT HAS USED ALL THOSE ADVANCES TO BRING A COURSE IN MIRACLES INTO THIS DREAM --

-- THE EGO HAS USED THOSE SAME ADVANCES TO MAKE THINGS LIKE NUCLEAR WEAPONS AND MATERIALISTIC SOCIETIES OF MEDIA DRIVEN CONSUMER OBJECT FETISHISM.

DRAWING OF: UNTITLED (I SHOP, THEREFORE I AM) © BARBARA KRUGER

THAT IS DUALITY FOR YOU. WHAT CAN BE USED TO ADVANCE THE HOLY SPIRIT'S SANITY CAN ALSO BE USED TO ADVANCE THE EGO'S INSANITY.

THAT INCLUDES A COURSE IN MIRACLES. REST ASSURED, IF GIVEN THE OPPORTUNITY, THE EGO WILL BE HAPPY TO DISTORT A COURSE IN MIRACLES FOR ITS OWN OBJECTIVES.

THE EGO WILL DISTORT THE COURSE SO PEOPLE WILL FEEL JUSTIFIED IN DISMISSING IT WITHOUT ANY SORT OF CONSISTENT UNDERSTANDING OF WHAT IT IS REALLY SAYING.

THIS IS TOO COMPLEX FOR A DUMB PERSON LIKE YOU. SO, JUST DISMISS IT AS NONSENSE.

THE EGO WILL DISTORT THE COURSE SO THAT PEOPLE WILL BE ABLE TO PRETEND TO DO THE COURSE WITHOUT ACTUALLY DOING SO.

FORGIVENESS IS ALL FINE, BUT YOU'VE GOT TO DRAW LIMITS.

AND TAKE IT EASY ON THIS ONENESS STUFF. LEAVE YOURSELF SOME DUALITY.

THE EGO WILL OVER-INTELLECTUALIZE THE COURSE AND MAKE IT SEEMINGLY IMPENETRABLE.

SPEND THE NEXT HOUR ARGUING OVER THE INTENDED MEANING OF THIS SENTENCE.

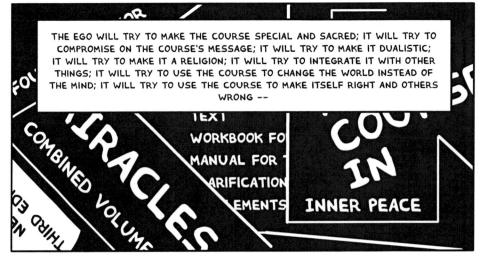

THE EGO WILL TRY TO MAKE THE COURSE SPECIAL AND SACRED; IT WILL TRY TO COMPROMISE ON THE COURSE'S MESSAGE; IT WILL TRY TO MAKE IT DUALISTIC; IT WILL TRY TO MAKE IT A RELIGION; IT WILL TRY TO INTEGRATE IT WITH OTHER THINGS; IT WILL TRY TO USE THE COURSE TO CHANGE THE WORLD INSTEAD OF THE MIND; IT WILL TRY TO USE THE COURSE TO MAKE ITSELF RIGHT AND OTHERS WRONG --

A BRIEF PERUSING OF A COURSE IN MIRACLES RELATED TALK ON THE INTERNET CAN PROVIDE NUMEROUS EXAMPLES OF THE EGO INSANITY BEHIND DISTORTING THE COURSE. BUT THAT IS WHAT THE EGO DOES, IT SPLITS AND DISTORTS. FORGIVE IT.

BROWSER

FILE EDIT VIEW HISTORY BOOKMARKS TOOLS HELP

  X ⌂ | HTTP://WWW.NONSEQUITURBABBLEBOARD.COM/BOARD

NON SEQUITUR BABBLE BOARD

| HOME | **BOARD** | MY ACCOUNT |

EVET47	I HEARD THAT THE SCRIBE OF THE COURSE WAS A MISERABLE ATHEIST, SO IT MUST NOT BE TRUE.
BILLKILLER	YEAH, I DON'T SEE HOW ANYTHING THAT TEACHES UNCOMPROMISING FORGIVENESS CAN BE ANYTHING BUT THE WORK OF SATAN.
PARANOIA66	PLUS, IT IS FISHY THAT BILL THETFORD SPENT SOME TIME WORKING FOR THE CIA.
FLAMING ATHEIST	YOU ARE ALL IDIOTS, THERE IS NO GOD OR JESUS OR SPAGHETTI MONSTER. I KNOW THIS PRECISELY BECAUSE I'VE NEVER HAD ANY MYSTICAL EXPERIENCES AND MY RATIONALIST MATERIALIST ROLE MODELS HAVEN'T EITHER.
ANIS	UNDOING THE EGO IS BRAIN WASHING. BUT THE WAY I THINK NOW IS NOT THE RESULT OF BRAIN WASHING SINCE I SHARE THE GENERAL THINKING OF THE WORLD.

⊞   ● BABBLE BOARD   🖳 ◖ 7:25 PM

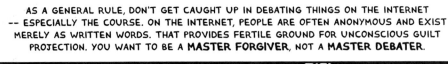

AS A GENERAL RULE, DON'T GET CAUGHT UP IN DEBATING THINGS ON THE INTERNET -- ESPECIALLY THE COURSE. ON THE INTERNET, PEOPLE ARE OFTEN ANONYMOUS AND EXIST MERELY AS WRITTEN WORDS. THAT PROVIDES FERTILE GROUND FOR UNCONSCIOUS GUILT PROJECTION. YOU WANT TO BE A **MASTER FORGIVER**, NOT A **MASTER DEBATER**.

164

THIS DREAM IS ALL SYMBOLIC AND THUS WORDS ARE SYMBOLS OF SYMBOLS MAKING WORDS TWICE REMOVED FROM REALITY. [2]

WORDS ARE TYPICAL EGO TOOLS IN THAT THEY FACILITATE COMMUNICATION BUT ALSO LIMIT COMMUNICATION. THAT IS WHY THERE ARE SO MANY LANGUAGES AND COLLOQUIALISMS IN THIS WORLD. AND THAT IS ALSO WHY WORDS ARE OFTEN USED TO EXPRESS NEGATIVE EMOTIONS AND INSTIGATE CONFLICT.

ACCEPT EXCEPT EXPECT ADAPT ADOPT ADVERSE AVERSE ADVICE ADVISE AFFECT EFFECT ALL READY ALREADY ALL RIGHT ALRIGHT ALL TOGETHER ALTOGETHER ALLUDE ELUDE ALLUSION ILLUSION A LOT MUCH MANY AMONG BETWEEN AMOUNT NUMBER ANXIOUS EAGER ANYPLACE ANYWHERE BECAUSE OF DUE TO BESIDE BESIDES BREATH BREATHE BUT HOWEVER YET CAN MAY CAPITAL CAPITOL CENSOR CENSURE CHOOSE CHOSE CHOSEN CITE SITE SIGHT CLOTHES CLOTHS COMPARE TO COMPARE WITH COMPLEMENT COMPLIMENT CONSCIENCE CONSCIOUS CONTINUAL CONTINUOUS COUNCIL COUNSEL DEPENDENT DEPENDANT DEVICE DEVISE DIFFERENT FROM DIFFERENT THAN DISINTERESTED UNINTERESTED ESPECIALLY SPECIALLY EVERYDAY EVERY DAY EVERYBODY EVERYONE EVERY ONE FARTHER FURTHER FORMALLY FORMERLY FORMER LATTER GOOD WELL HANGED HUNG HEALTHFUL HEALTHY HEAR HERE HOPING HOPPING IMPLY INFER IN INTO ITS IT'S LAY LIE NAUSEA NAUSEATED NAUSEATING NAUSEOUS PASSED PAST PERSPECTIVE PROSPECTIVE PRECEDE PROCEED PRINCIPAL PRINCIPLE QUOTATION QUOTE QUIET QUIT QUITE REAL REALLY VERY SHERBET SHERBERT SOME TIME SOMETIME SOMETIMES STATIONARY STATIONERY SUPPOSED TO USED TO THAN THEN THEIR THERE THEY'RE 'TIL TILL UNTIL TO TOO TWO AS AS IF LIKE ASSURE ENSURE INSURE AWFUL AWFULLY AWHILE A WHILE BAD BADLY LEAD LED LOOSE LOSE MANY MUCH MAY BE MAYBE MORAL MORALE USAGE USE WERE WE'RE WHERE WHICH WHO THAT WHOSE WHO'S YOUR YOU'RE

A COURSE IN MIRACLES ITSELF USES WORDS, WHICH ARE SYMBOLIC, AND CANNOT EXPRESS WHAT LIES BEYOND SYMBOLS. THE COURSE REMAINS WITHIN THE EGO FRAMEWORK, WHERE IT IS NEEDED. [3]

THE COURSE IS WRITTEN POETICALLY, MUCH OF WHICH IS IN **IAMBIC PENTAMETER**, WHICH, IN UNRHYMED FORM, IS KNOWN AS SHAKESPEAREAN BLANK VERSE. NOT ONLY DOES THE COURSE'S POETIC USE OF LANGUAGE MAKE IT MORE ARTISTIC AND SONGLIKE, BUT IT ALSO MAKES THE COURSE MORE TIMELESS.

DA DUM ⟶ NO ONE
DA DUM ⟶ WHO HATES
DA DUM ⟶ BUT IS
DA DUM ⟶ AFRAID
DA DUM ⟶ OF LOVE

WHICH IS ALSO WHY THE COURSE USES A LOT OF TRADITIONAL JUDEO-CHRISTIAN TERMINOLOGY, BUT REDEFINES IT.

GOD
PRONUNCIATION: GÄD ALSO GÒD
FUNCTION: NOUN

1 CONVENTIONAL DEFINITION: THE BEING PERFECT IN POWER, WISDOM, AND GOODNESS WHO IS NONETHELESS CREDITED AS THE CREATOR AND RULER OF THIS UNIVERSE.

2 A COURSE IN MIRACLES DEFINITION: THE FIRST CAUSE WHOSE EFFECT IS CHRIST AND WHOSE REALITY IS THAT OF PURE ONENESS.

HUNDREDS TO THOUSANDS OF YEARS IN THE FUTURE, PEOPLE WILL STILL BE READING THE BIBLE AND STILL BE READING SHAKESPEARE, THUS THE COURSE USES THAT SAME KIND OF TIME TRANSCENDING LANGUAGE.

THE COURSE'S LANGUAGE FORCES READERS TO SLOW DOWN AND REALLY **ABSORB** THE WORDS. SOME PEOPLE COMPLAIN ABOUT THAT.

AND SOME PEOPLE COMPLAIN ABOUT OTHER THINGS, LIKE THE COURSE'S USE OF MALE SPECIFIC WORDS. BUT THE EGO LIKES TO COMPLAIN ABOUT A LOT OF THINGS -- ESPECIALLY THINGS THAT ARE DESIGNED TO UNDO THE EGO. FORGIVE Y'SHUA FOR NOT BEING CONCERNED WITH FREEDOM STIFLING TRENDS IN POLITICAL CORRECTNESS.

ALTHOUGH THE TRUTH IS SIMPLE, THE EGO IS NOT. SO, UNDOING THE EGO TAKES SOME DETAIL.

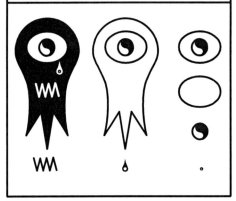

THE COURSE CONSISTS OF THREE BOOKS IN ONE BOOK: A 622-PAGE **TEXT**, A 478-PAGE **WORKBOOK FOR STUDENTS**, AND AN 88-PAGE **MANUAL FOR TEACHERS**. IN ADDITION, THERE ARE TWO SUPPLEMENTS TO THE COURSE: **THE SONG OF PRAYER** AND **THE PSYCHOTHERAPY PAMPHLET**.

THE TEXT LAYS OUT THE PURE NONDUALISTIC METAPHYSICS OF THE COURSE IN PREPARATION FOR THE WORKBOOK FOR STUDENTS.

THE WORKBOOK FOR STUDENTS PRESENTS 365 LESSONS THAT PUT THE METAPHYSICS OF THE COURSE'S TEXT TO EXPERIENTIAL APPLICATION. THE LESSONS HELP STUDENTS LEARN HOW TO TURN TO THE HOLY SPIRIT.

166

THEN FINALLY, THE MANUAL FOR TEACHERS PRESENTS A SERIES OF QUESTIONS AND ANSWERS THAT SUMMARIZE THE COURSE AND HELP STUDENTS BECOME TRUE TEACHERS OF GOD.

SKELETON KEY TO READING A COURSE IN MIRACLES

ANYTHING TALKING ABOUT DUALITY IS METAPHOR.

METAPHOR EXAMPLE: GOD WEEPS...GOD IS LONELY.

ANYTHING TALKING ABOUT NONDUALITY IS LITERAL.

NONDUALITY EXAMPLE: GOD IS.

THE COURSE WORKBOOK TAKES A MINIMUM OF ONE YEAR TO COMPLETE. THE WORKBOOK HELPS GET STUDENTS TUNED INTO THE HOLY SPIRIT. AND ONLY BY TUNING INTO THE HOLY SPIRIT CAN A STUDENT TRULY BECOME A TEACHER OF GOD.

ACCORDING TO A COURSE IN MIRACLES, TO TEACH IS TO LEARN SO THAT TEACHER AND LEARNER ARE THE SAME. [4]

VOLUME

84 88 92 94 96 98 100 104 106 108

TUNING

TEACHING IS A CONSTANT PROCESS AND WE ARE ALL ALWAYS EITHER TEACHING THE EGO THOUGHT SYSTEM OR THE HOLY SPIRIT THOUGHT SYSTEM -- DEPENDING ON WHO WE ARE CHOOSING AS OUR TEACHER.

SO, IN THAT SENSE, EVERYONE IS A TEACHER. THEREFORE, TRUE TEACHING IS NOT DOING THINGS LIKE GIVING LECTURES ON VARIOUS SUBJECTS, TRUE TEACHING IS DEMONSTRATING EITHER RIGHT-MINDEDNESS OR WRONG-MINDEDNESS THROUGH NORMAL EVERYDAY ACTION.

TO TRULY TEACH THE HOLY SPIRIT'S THOUGHT SYSTEM, YOU MUST TRULY CHOOSE THE HOLY SPIRIT AS YOUR TEACHER. OTHERWISE, YOU CAN'T HELP BUT TEACH THE EGO'S CURRICULUM. WHAT YOU DO IS A RESULT OF WHAT YOU THINK.

NO ONE REALLY NEEDS TO TEACH A COURSE IN MIRACLES ITSELF, THE COURSE ITSELF DOES THAT. HOWEVER, THE COURSE CAN BE DAUNTING WITHOUT FIRST RECEIVING A SUFFICIENT INTRODUCTION.

MY OWN INTRODUCTION TO A COURSE IN MIRACLES CAME BY WAY OF A BOOK TITLED **THE DISAPPEARANCE OF THE UNIVERSE**.

I WENT TO CATHOLIC SCHOOL FOR MOST OF MY EDUCATION. SO, BY THE TIME I WAS IN HIGH SCHOOL, I WAS FAMILIAR ENOUGH WITH CHRISTIANITY AND RELIGION IN GENERAL TO KNOW, FROM AN INSIDER'S POINT OF VIEW, THAT IT DIDN'T MAKE MUCH SENSE TO ME.

FUN TIP: WHEN SHAKING HANDS WITH PEOPLE, TICKLE THEIR PALM WITH YOUR INDEX FINGER. THIS IS ESPECIALLY FUN TO DO DURING THE SIGN OF PEACE AT CATHOLIC MASS.

THERE WAS A MYSTICAL AND ART HISTORICAL ASPECT TO THE CATHOLIC CHURCH THAT MADE IT MORE APPEALING TO ME THAN OTHER RELIGIONS, ESPECIALLY FUNDAMENTALIST FORMS OF CHRISTIANITY --

HAIL MARY FULL OF GRACE, PLEASE DON'T LET ME HAVE ANY VISIONS OF YOU, LIKE IN FATIMA. ALSO, DON'T LET ME GET STIGMATA. AND, OH YEAH, DON'T LET ME END UP LIKE LINDA BLAIR.

POLITICS WERE A HOPELESS SHAM.

PSYCHOLOGY WAS INCONSISTENT.

ALTERNATIVE SPIRITUALITY WAS A WEB OF CONFUSION.

AND EVEN THE COMMON PURSUITS IN LIFE -- LIKE MONEY, ROMANCE, AND BEER -- PROVED TO ME TO BE MISERABLE AND POINTLESS.

I JUST DON'T LIKE YOU IN THAT WAY.

I FIGURED THAT I HAD TWO CHOICES. EITHER I COULD SLAM MY HEAD AGAINST THE WALL UNTIL I SUFFERED ENOUGH BRAIN DAMAGE TO BECOME A COMMON, ROBOTIC, HALFWIT CONSUMER OF THE GARBAGE HANDED DOWN FROM ON HIGH BY THE CLUELESS SOULS WHO OCCUPY THE UPPER ECHELONS OF THE SOCIOECONOMIC MACHINERY --

WOW! THIS MUSIC WON A GRAMMY? THEN IT MUST BE GOOD.

170

AS I CONTINUED SEARCHING, I LEARNED PLENTY OF INTERESTING STUFF, BUT IT ALL SIMPLY LEFT ME **HAUNTED** BY TWO SIMILAR AND EQUALLY HOPELESS IDEAS.

THE ONE IDEA WAS A MIX OF MISCELLANEOUS NEW AGE GIBBERISH THAT I CALLED **THE MADNESS OF INFINITIES**.

3.14159265358979323846264338327950288419716939937
510582097494459230781640628620899862803482534
211706798214808651328230664709384460955058223172
535940812848111745028410270193852110555964446229
489549303819644288109756659334461284756482337867
831652712019091456485669234603486104543266482133
939360726024914127372458700660631558817488152092
096282925409171536436789259036001133053054882046
652138414695194151160943305727036575959195309214
061171183192611793105118548074462379962749567351885
752724891227938183011949129833673362440656641308
602139494639522473719070217986094370277053921717
629317675238467481846766940513200056812714526356
082778577134275778960917363717872146844090122495
349430146549585337105079227968925892354209956112
902196086403441815981362977477130996051870721134
999998372978049951059731732816096318595024459455
346908302642522308253344685035261931188171010
003137838752886587533208381420617177669147303598
253490428755468731159562863882353787593751957781
857780532171226806613001927876611195909216420198
938095257201065485863278865936153381827968230301
952035301852968995773622599413891249721775283479
313515574857242454150695950829533116861727855889

IT WAS THE IDEA THAT I'M IMMORTAL AND I HAVE SOME KIND OF MENTAL CONTROL OVER THINGS IN THIS UNIVERSE, BUT I DON'T REALLY HAVE ANY DEFINITIVE PLACE TO GO, SO IT IS ALL KIND OF PERPETUALLY POINTLESS -- AS IF I'M SENTENCED LIKE THE MYTHICAL **SISYPHUS** TO ETERNALLY ROLL A ROCK UP A HILL ONLY TO LET IT ROLL DOWN AGAIN.

DEATH DIDN'T EVEN OFFER AN ESCAPE FROM THAT QUANDARY.

THE OTHER IDEA WAS A SURRENDER TO MATERIALISM THAT I CALLED **THE APPEAL OF NIHILISM**.

ALEX AS NIETZSCHE

IT WAS THE MODERN AESTHETIC EXISTENTIALIST IDEA OFTEN EXPRESSED IN THE MATERIALISTIC TRUISM THAT WE ARE MADE OF **STARDUST** -- SUGGESTING THAT WE ARE MERELY PHYSICAL CREATURES THAT AROSE AS SOME KIND OF WEIRD COSMIC FLUKE AND WE ARE DAMN LUCKY, OR UNLUCKY, TO BE HERE.

AT LEAST DEATH OFFERED AN ESCAPE FROM THAT POINTLESS SITUATION. BUT MY OWN PRIMARY EXPERIENCE IN MY OWN MIND OF BEING SOMETHING NON-MATERIAL MADE THAT IDEA SEEM JUST AS RIDICULOUS AND WRONG MINDED TO ME AS THE IDEA THAT JESUS WAS SENT ON A SUICIDE MISSION TO EARTH BY GOD TO ATONE FOR HUMANITY'S SINS.

SO, ALTHOUGH I WAS DISCOURAGED, I CARRIED ON WITH MY SEARCH, BECAUSE I WASN'T READY TO REVERT TO BRAIN DAMAGE.

BUT, AT THAT POINT, I WAS BECOMING BURNT OUT; THE SO-CALLED KNOWLEDGE OF THIS WORLD JUST SEEMED SO CLUELESS AND INCOMPLETE. I WAS BEGINNING TO COME TO THE CONCLUSION THAT NOTHING IN THIS WORLD CAN TRULY BE KNOWN. THUS, I WAS READY TO START UNLEARNING.

NOTE: SO-CALLED EDUCATION IN THIS ILLUSORY UNIVERSE IS MERELY LEARNING HOW TO JUDGE WHICH ILLUSIONS ARE GOOD, TRUE, BAD, OR FALSE.

172

FORTUNATELY, I FINALLY CAME ACROSS A COMPREHENSIVE BOOK ABOUT A COURSE IN MIRACLES TITLED **THE DISAPPEARANCE OF THE UNIVERSE** BY GARY RENARD.

THE DISAPPEARANCE OF THE UNIVERSE IS A BOOK (PUBLISHED IN 2003) THAT RECOUNTS SEVENTEEN CONVERSATIONS (STARTING IN 1992) THAT WERE CENTERED AROUND A COURSE IN MIRACLES AND TOOK PLACE BETWEEN GARY RENARD AND TWO ASCENDED MASTERS NAMED ARTEN AND PURSAH.

AT FIRST, I WAS SKEPTICAL OF THE BOOK -- MOSTLY DUE TO ITS PREMISE. I FIGURED THAT IT WOULD BE A BUNCH OF TYPICAL NONSENSE WITH A FEW INTERESTING THOUGHTS, BUT WITHOUT ANY COHERENT PICTURE OR DEFINITIVE OBJECTIVE.

HOWEVER, BY THE TIME I WAS HALF WAY THROUGH THE BOOK, I REALIZED THAT A COURSE IN MIRACLES WAS EXACTLY WHAT I HAD BEEN LOOKING FOR.

WITHIN 24 HOURS OF STARTING THE BOOK, I FINISHED IT AND STARTED READING IT AGAIN.

IT BASICALLY ANSWERED ALL MY QUESTIONS AND MADE TOTAL SENSE TO ME; I FELT AS IF I HAD FINALLY BEEN REMINDED OF SOMETHING I HAD LONG WANTED TO REMEMBER.

ONE OF THE GREAT THINGS ABOUT A COURSE IN MIRACLES IS THAT IT IS A PRIVATE SELF-STUDY COURSE THAT DOESN'T REQUIRE CHANGING ANYTHING EXCEPT YOUR **MIND**. IT ISN'T CONCERNED WITH WHAT YOU DO EXTERNALLY.

A COURSE IN MIRACLES IS ALWAYS DONE AT THE LEVEL OF THE MIND BECAUSE MIND IS THE **CAUSE** OF EVERYTHING; THE PHYSICAL DREAM WORLD IS THE EFFECT. WHAT YOU DO IS THE RESULT OF WHAT YOU THINK. AND WHAT YOU THINK DETERMINES YOUR EXPERIENCE IN THIS DREAM.

WHETHER YOU ARE A GAY ASSASSIN OR A CELIBATE CHARITY WORKER, THE COURSE DOESN'T CARE; IT MEETS YOU WHERE YOU THINK YOU ARE.

THE COURSE PASSES NO JUDGMENT UPON FORM; INSTEAD, IT MERELY ASKS WHAT THE FORM IS FOR SYMBOLICALLY, WHICH EMPHASIZES ITS CONTENT AND THUS FACILITATES FORGIVENESS.

A COURSE IN MIRACLES COMBINED

PREFACE

TEXT

WORKBOOK FOR STUDENTS

MANUAL FOR TEACHERS

CLARIFICATION OF TERMS

SUPPLEMENTS

THE COURSE IS THE SHORTEST PATH AVAILABLE OUT OF THIS DREAM. YET, IT IS STILL A LIFELONG PATH; IT ISN'T JUST SOME BOOK YOU READ AND THAT IS IT -- ALTHOUGH SUCH A SCENARIO CERTAINLY ISN'T IMPOSSIBLE.

FOUN

IF YOU WERE SHOWN ALL YOUR UNCONSCIOUS GUILT ALL AT ONCE AND ASKED TO TRULY FORGIVE IT, IT WOULD SCARE THE HELL BACK OUT OF YOU AND INTO THIS DREAM. I KNOW THAT FROM EXPERIENCE.

THE REAL REAL WORLD IS THE DREAM SEEN AS A SYMBOL OF HEAVEN, PERCEIVED THROUGH THE EYES OF A FULLY HEALED, **GUILTLESS MIND**, WHERE PERCEPTION IS THAT OF PURE FORGIVENESS AND TOTAL JOINING.

ATTAINMENT OF THE REAL REAL WORLD IS THE END OF OUR INDIVIDUAL PATHS BACK HOME TO ONENESS.

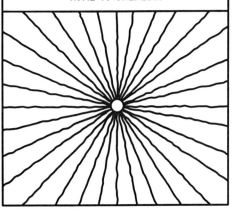

AT THAT POINT, WE BREAK FREE OF THE SELF-IMPOSED CONFINES OF SPACETIME AND USHER IN THE TRUE MEANING OF THE **SECOND COMING**: OUR FRAGMENTED MIND IS REJOINED IN AWARENESS TO OUR ONE WHOLE MIND: CHRIST.

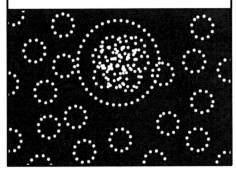

THAT THEN USHERS IN THE TRUE MEANING OF THE **FINAL JUDGMENT** AND THE **APOCALYPSE**: WE SEPARATE TRUTH FROM ILLUSION ONCE AND FOR ALL AND UNDO OUR INITIAL JUDGMENT, WHICH CONDEMNED US TO DREAMS OF HELL BY PLACING A HEAVY VEIL OF GUILT OVER LOVE.

THEN FINALLY, THE LAST STEP ON OUR JOURNEY IS TAKEN METAPHORICALLY BY GOD. AND AT THAT POINT, WE RETURN TO HEAVEN, WHICH WE NEVER LEFT.

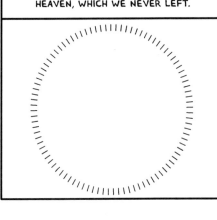

IN THIS DREAM, EACH OF OUR SEEMINGLY SEPARATE MINDS IS LIKE A UNIQUE SHADE OF COLOR.

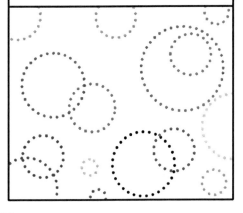

178

BUT OUR RETURN TO HEAVEN IS LIKE MERGING INTO ONE WHOLE, PURE, PERFECT WHITE LIGHT THAT BLENDS SEAMLESSLY INTO THE PERFECT LIGHT OF GOD.

PRISM
OF
FORGIVENESS

IF ANY INFINITESIMALLY TINY SHADE OF ANY COLOR IS MISSING FROM THAT LIGHT, IT IS NOT PERFECT WHITE LIGHT. THEREFORE, WE CAN'T LEAVE ANYONE OUT. WHICH MEANS OUR FORGIVENESS MUST BE PERFECT.

PRISM
OF
FORGIVENESS

ONCE WE MELT AWAY THE LAST **SPECK** OF GUILT FROM OUR MIND, THEN THAT IS THE END OF THIS DREAM. THIS DREAM TOTALLY VANISHES WITHOUT ANY MEMORY OF IT EVER EXISTING -- SINCE IT NEVER REALLY DID EXIST.

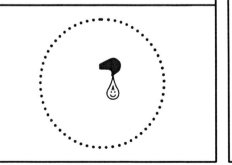

GOD IS AND NOTHING ELSE IS, JUST LIKE IT HAS ALWAYS BEEN, EVEN WHILE WE SEEMED TO BE LOST IN ILLUSIONS.

179

IF YOU DIDN'T LIKE THIS BOOK, THEN TAKE IT UP WITH THE **HOLY SPIRIT**. THE HOLY SPIRIT IS RESPONSIBLE FOR THIS BOOK, NOT ME.

LOOK INSIDE

THE UNIVERSE IS A DREAM (PAPERBACK)

ALEXANDER MARCHAND (AUTHOR)

★★★★★

PRICE: TOO EXPENSIVE TO SHOW

IN STOCK

THE UNIVERSE IS A DREAM

ALEXANDER MARCHAND

CUSTOMER REVIEWS

LEAST HELPFUL CUSTOMER REVIEW
2 OF 734 PEOPLE FOUND THE FOLLOWING REVIEW HELPFUL:
★☆☆☆☆   **I WANT TO MURDER ALEX!!!**
BY PROJECTOR — SEE ALL MY NEGATIVE REVIEWS
    FAKE NAME

I DIDN'T ACTUALLY BUY THE BOOK AND I ONLY LOOKED AT THE FIRST 3 PAGES, BUT I CAN TELL THAT I HATE THIS BOOK; IT CHALLENGES MY CHERISHED EGO BELIEFS WAY TOO MUCH.

NEWEST REVIEWS
7 OF 8 PEOPLE FOUND THE FOLLOWING REVIEW HELPFUL:
★★★★★   **A HAPPY SUPRISE!**
BY RRGUY — SEE ALL MY SUPRISED REVIEWS
    FAKE NAME

I ORDERED THE BOOK "HOW TO BUILD YOUR UNIVERSE WITH MODEL TRAINS," BUT SPAM SENT ME THIS INSTEAD. FORTUNATELY THO THE BOOK WAS GREAT!

1 OF 12 PEOPLE FOUND THE FOLLOWING REVIEW HELPFUL:
★☆☆☆☆   **TOO NONDUALISTIC**
BY STUNTED FORGIVER — SEE ALL MY DISGRUNTLED REVIEW
    FAKE NAME

I'VE BEEN AN ACIM STUDENT FOR 20 YEARS AN I PREFER TO STICK WITH MY OWN DUALISTIC INTERPRETATION OF IT.

IF YOU TAKE IT UP WITH THE HOLY SPIRIT, YOU'LL BE GUIDED TO USE YOUR DISMAY AS AN OPPORTUNITY TO PRACTICE **TRUE FORGIVENESS**. AND TRUE FORGIVENESS IS WHAT IT IS ALL ABOUT.

COMPLAINT DEPARTMENT

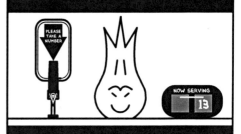

PLEASE TAKE A NUMBER

NOW SERVING 13

THE FACT IS THAT THE SCRIPT IS WRITTEN; IT IS NO ACCIDENT THAT YOU FOUND AND READ THIS BOOK. YOU DREAMT THIS BOOK UP BECAUSE NOW IS YOUR TIME TO GET TO WAKING. THERE IS NO POINT IN DELAY.

SO, ALTHOUGH IT IS TIME TO SAY GOODBYE FOR NOW, THIS IS NOT REALLY THE END, BUT MERELY THE BEGINNING OF THE END. THIS IS THE BEGINNING OF A NEW WAY OF LOOKING.

IF THE IDEAS IN THIS BOOK HAVE BEEN NEW TO YOU, THEN YOU SHOULD GET TO WORK READING THIS BOOK AGAIN, AND AGAIN. BECAUSE IT IS SAFE TO SAY THAT THE EGO MADE YOU MISS AND DISTORT A LOT OF ESSENTIAL INFORMATION.

NEVER UNDERESTIMATE THE POWER OF DENIAL. DENIAL IS WHAT MADE THIS UNIVERSE AFTER ALL.

BEYOND REREADING THIS BOOK, YOU WOULD ALSO BE WISE TO OBTAIN A COURSE IN MIRACLES -- THAT IS, IF YOU DON'T ALREADY HAVE IT.

THIS BOOK IS MERELY A BRIEF SAMPLING OF THE DEEP INSIGHTS AVAILABLE IN A COURSE IN MIRACLES. SO, IF YOU WANT TO GO DEEPER, YOU NEED A COURSE IN MIRACLES.

OTHER THAN THAT ADVICE, I CAN'T EXACTLY TELL YOU WHAT TO DO NEXT. EACH PATH HOME TO ONENESS IS HIGHLY INDIVIDUALIZED, BECAUSE THE EGO IS HIGHLY INDIVIDUALIZED.

NOTE: IF YOU ARE READING THIS BOOK IN THE FUTURE AND I HAVE MADE SEQUEL BOOKS TO THIS BOOK, THEN BY ALL MEANS READ THOSE BOOKS NEXT.

THERE IS NO UNIVERSAL **THEOLOGY**, ONLY A UNIVERSAL **EXPERIENCE**. [5] WHICH MAKES SENSE, BECAUSE, FOR EXAMPLE, DOG MINDS OBVIOUSLY CAN'T READ AND STUDY SOMETHING LIKE A COURSE IN MIRACLES. YET, ALL DOG MINDS ARE NONETHELESS DESTINED TO AWAKEN, AND THAT IS BECAUSE ALL MINDS ARE DESTINED TO EVENTUALLY TURN AWAY FROM THE EGO AND TO THE HOLY SPIRIT.

ONLY BY TURNING AWAY FROM THE EGO WILL YOU BEGIN TO AWAKEN. AND IN THAT PROCESS YOU'LL BE ABLE TO EXPERIENTIALLY VERIFY THE ACCURACY OF THE IDEAS IN THIS BOOK.

RIGHT

WRONG

I CAN'T SAY WAKING UP WILL BE EASY. THE FACT IS THAT THE EGO IS NOT GOING TO GO DOWN WITHOUT A FIGHT.

JUST **LOOK** AT THE EGO, DON'T FIGHT IT.

OH, A WISE GUY EH?

PRISONERS BOUND WITH HEAVY CHAINS FOR YEARS, STARVED AND EMACIATED, WEAK AND EXHAUSTED, AND WITH EYES SO LONG CAST DOWN IN DARKNESS THEY REMEMBER NOT THE LIGHT, DO NOT LEAP UP IN JOY THE INSTANT THEY ARE MADE FREE. IT TAKES A WHILE FOR THEM TO UNDERSTAND WHAT FREEDOM IS. [6]

SO, YOU MAY POINTLESSLY DELAY PUTTING TO PRACTICE THE IDEAS IN THIS BOOK, BUT ONCE YOU START THIS JOURNEY, THE END IS CERTAIN.

I'LL TALK TO YOU LATER. FOREVER ONE!

A WAY A LONE A LAST A LOVED A LONG THE...

ALEX READING EVERYONE'S WAKE

ALEX

GET THE WORD OUT
IF YOU ENJOYED THIS BOOK, TELL OTHERS
ABOUT IT.

TO BE
CONTINUED...

MAP OF TIME

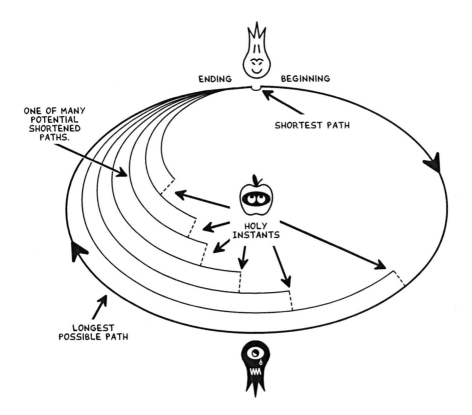

ENDING BEGINNING

ONE OF MANY
POTENTIAL
SHORTENED
PATHS.

SHORTEST PATH

HOLY
INSTANTS

LONGEST
POSSIBLE PATH

GLOSSARY OF SYMBOLS

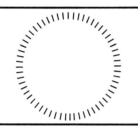

GOD
A CIRCLE HAS NO BEGINNING AND NO END, LIKE GOD. CONSEQUENTLY, GOD IS REPRESENTED BY A CIRCLE. BUT THE CIRCLE ISN'T A REGULAR CIRCLE, IT IS A RADIATING CIRCLE MADE OF THIN LINES, SUGGESTING EXTENSION, LIGHT, AND ABSTRACTION.

MIND
MIND IS THE CREATIVE ELEMENT OF SPIRIT, WHICH COMES FROM GOD. CONSEQUENTLY, LIKE GOD, MIND IS ALSO REPRESENTED BY A CIRCLE. BUT THE CIRCLE FOR MIND IS A DOTTED CIRCLE.

HOLY SPIRIT/RIGHT MIND
THE HOLY SPIRIT IS REPRESENTED BY A GHOST-LIKE HAPPY FLAME, SUGGESTING LIGHT AND SPIRIT.

EGO/WRONG MIND
THE EGO IS REPRESENTED BY A MONSTER-LIKE ENTITY WITH A SINGLE, LARGE, PENETRATING EYE, SUGGESTING CONSCIOUSNESS. THE SHAPE OF THE EGO SYMBOL IS THE INVERSION OF THE SHAPE OF THE HOLY SPIRIT SYMBOL.

FORGIVENESS
FORGIVENESS IS REPRESENTED BY A HAPPY DROP OF WATER, WHICH SUGGESTS CLEANSING AS WELL AS MELTING.

185

FAKE FORGIVENESS

FAKE FORGIVENESS IS REPRESENTED BY AN INVERSION OF THE SYMBOL FOR TRUE FORGIVENESS. THE SHAPE SUGGESTS A SPEAR. AND THE EYEBALL SUGGESTS THE DUALITY INHERENT IN CONSCIOUSNESS.

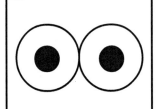

CONSCIOUSNESS

CONSCIOUSNESS IS REPRESENTED BY LARGE, ROUND EYES. THE GAZE OF THE EYES SUGGESTS THE SPLIT BETWEEN SUBJECT AND OBJECT, OBSERVER AND OBSERVED.

UNCONSCIOUSNESS

UNCONSCIOUSNESS IS REPRESENTED BY AN ICEBERG WHOSE GAZING EYES AT THE SURFACE ARE BLIND TO THE MASS BENEATH THE WATER.

SIN/PAST

SIN IS REPRESENTED BY EYES HIDING IN AN APPLE LOOKING TO THE LEFT, SUGGESTING THE PAST. THE APPLE SYMBOL IS BORROWED FROM THE ADAM AND EVE CREATION MYTH TO REPRESENT GUILT. THE PAST TENSE OF GUILT IS SIN.

GUILT/PRESENT

GUILT IS REPRESENTED BY EYES HIDING IN AN APPLE LOOKING STRAIGHT AHEAD SUGGESTING GUILT IN THE PRESENT TENSE. THE APPLE SYMBOL IS BORROWED FROM THE ADAM AND EVE CREATION MYTH TO REPRESENT GUILT.

FEAR/FUTURE

FEAR IS REPRESENTED BY EYES HIDING IN AN APPLE LOOKING TO THE RIGHT, SUGGESTING THE FUTURE. THE APPLE SYMBOL IS BORROWED FROM THE ADAM AND EVE CREATION MYTH TO REPRESENT GUILT. THE FUTURE TENSE OF GUILT IS FEAR.

HOLY INSTANT
THE HOLY INSTANT IS REPRESENTED BY EYES HIDING IN AN APPLE LOOKING UPWARD TO THE DIVINE, SUGGESTING THE TRANSCENDENCE OF TIME AND THE DISSOLVING OF UNCONSCIOUS GUILT.

SPECIAL LOVE
SPECIAL LOVE IS REPRESENTED BY TWO DIFFERENT HALVES OF A HEART ATTEMPTING TO JOIN AS ONE, SUGGESTING THE ATTEMPT TO JOIN OUT OF A SENSE OF INCOMPLETENESS, WHICH EXCLUDES THE WHOLE IN FAVOR OF A TINY POCKET OF SPECIAL ISOLATION. THE EYEBALLS REPRESENT THE SUBJECT OBJECT SPLIT OF CONSCIOUSNESS.

SPECIAL HATE
SPECIAL HATE IS REPRESENTED BY TWO DIFFERENT HALVES OF A HEART TURNED AWAY FROM EACH OTHER, SUGGESTING THE REFUSAL TO JOIN. THE EYEBALLS REPRESENT THE SUBJECT OBJECT SPLIT OF CONSCIOUSNESS.

HOLY LOVE
HOLY LOVE IS REPRESENTED BY AN UNDIVIDED HEART WITH EYES FIXED UPWARD UPON THE DIVINE. THIS SUGGESTS A DISSOLVING OF THE UNCONSCIOUS AND THUS A DISSOLVING OF OTHERNESS INTO ONENESS.

MIRACLE
A MIRACLE IS REPRESENTED BY A STAR WITH EYES FIXED UPWARD UPON THE DIVINE, SUGGESTING ILLUMINATION, TRANSCENDENCE, AND THE DISSOLVING OF THE UNCONSCIOUS. MIRACLES UNITE US WITH OUR ONE WHOLE MIND.

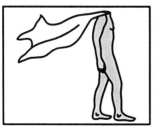

THE HERO OF THE DREAM
THE HERO OF THE DREAM IS THE BODY. CONSEQUENTLY, THE HERO OF THE DREAM IS REPRESENTED BY A HEADLESS BODY WEARING A SUPERHERO CAPE. THE HEADLESSNESS SUGGESTS AN ABSENCE OF MIND AND SPIRIT, THUS EMPHASIZING THE PHYSICAL.

187

DUALITY
DUALITY IS REPRESENTED BY THE YIN YANG SYMBOL
(TAIJITU).

DUALISTIC THOUGHT
DUALISTIC THOUGHT IS REPRESENTED BY CLOUDS
INTERPOSED WITH THE DUALITY SYMBOL.

PROJECTION
PROJECTION IS REPRESENTED BY A FILM PROJECTOR PLAYING
FILMS OF DUALISTIC THOUGHT.

188

INDEX OF REFERENCES

TO *A COURSE IN MIRACLES*
USED WITH CONSENT FROM THE ORIGINAL PUBLISHER: THE FOUNDATION FOR INNER PEACE
WWW.ACIM.COM

BOOK KEY

T TEXT
W WORKBOOK FOR STUDENT
M MANUAL FOR TEACHERS
P PSYCHOTHERAPY PAMPHLET
S SONG OF PRAYER PAMPHLET
C CLARIFICATION OF TERMS

EXAMPLE

T.1.V.1.1
BOOK.CHAPTER.SECTION.PARAGRAPH.SENTENCE

CHAPTER ZERO

1 (T.1.VI.4.4)

CHAPTER ONE NINTH

1 (W.P1.105.4.3)

CHAPTER THREE NINTHS

1 (T.30.III.6), 2 (T.19.IV.C.1), 3 (T.2.I.1.9), 4 (T.21.IN.1), 5 (T.18.VII.3), 6 (T.26.VIII.1.4)

CHAPTER FOUR NINTHS

1 (T.23.II.2), 2 (T.23.II.20), 3 (T.5.V.5.1), 4 (T.16.II.3), 5 (T.20.VI.11.1), 6 (T.4.V.4),
7 (T.27.VIII), 8 (T.16.V.6), 9 (T.16.VI.4), 10 (T.15.VII.8), 11 (19.IV.B.14), 12 (T.13.II.5.6),
13 (T.13.II.6), 14 (T.21.IV.3.3), 15 (T.13.II.7), 16 (T.13.II.9.2)

CHAPTER FIVE NINTHS

1 (T.19.IV), 2 (T.1.V.2.2), 3 (T.22.3), 4 (P.2.IV.1.7), 5 (T.26.V.13.1), 6 (W.P1.26.7.4),
7 (W.P1.56.1.1), 8 (W.P1.201.1), 9 (T.3.VII.6.11), 10 (T.6.I.4.4), 11 (T.6.I.13.2), 12 (W.P1.68.1.1),
13 (T.12.I.8.13), 14 (T.1.I.45.2), 15 (T.IN.2), 16 (T.11.V.9)

CHAPTER SIX NINTHS

1 (T.13.IN.2), 2 (T.13.IN.3), 3 (T.26.VII.4.7), 4 (T.2.IV.2), 5 (T.5.V.5.3), 6 (P.2.VI.1),
7 (T.31.VIII.1.5), 8 (T.4.II.7), 9 (T.1.VII.3.6), 10 (T.20.II.1), 11 (19.IV.B.3)

CHAPTER SEVEN NINTHS

1 (S.1.IN.1.3), 2 (S.1.II.1.5), 3 (T.9.II.1.1), 4 (T.3.V.6.3), 5 (S.2.IN.13), 6 (T.26.VI.1), 7 (S.1.I.4.2),
8 (T.30.I.1), 9 (T.30.I.14) 10 (T.16.V.3)

CHAPTER EIGHT NINTHS

1 (T.18.VII.4.4), 2 (M.21.1.9), 3 (C.IN.3.1), 4 (M.IN.1.5), 5 (C.IN.2.5), 6 (T.20.III.9)

AND I GET LETTERS...

DEAR ALEX,
MY NAME IS SANDY. I'M A BIG FAN OF ALL YOUR STUFF. MY FRIENDS AND I LOVE YOU. WHEN ARE YOU GOING TO VISIT PHILADELPHIA? YOU CAN STAY WITH ME! THAT WOULD BE SO FUN! BUT ANYWAY, I WAS JUST WONDERING WHY YOU HAVE A BLACK DOT ON YOUR HEAD IN YOUR COMICS. I HAVE THEORIES, BUT I WANTED TO ASK YOU AND FIND OUT FOR SURE.
SINCERELY, SANDY
PHILADELPHIA, PA

DEAR SANDY,
THANKS FOR THE LETTER. CAN I STAY AT YOUR HOUSE FOR ABOUT 9 MONTHS STARTING IN OCTOBER? JUST KIDDING. THE BLACK DOT IS A LITTLE MOLE I HAVE ON MY FOREHEAD. SOME PEOPLE CALL IT MY NATURAL THIRD EYE (SPIRITUAL EYE). IN A PRACTICAL SENSE, THE MOLE HELPS DIFFERENTIATE ME FROM MY EVIL TWIN ZELA. ZELA USUALLY WEARS HIS BANGS DOWN SO PEOPLE WILL THINK HE'S ME. DON'T LET HIM FOOL YOU!
YOUR FRIEND, ALEX

GOOD DAY, MATE!
MY NAME IS JOHN. I'VE BEEN CAUGHT UP IN THE WHOLE MANIFESTING INTENTIONS TREND FOR A FEW YEARS NOW, WITH ONLY MEAGER RESULTS. YOU SEEM TO CALL MANIFESTING INTENTIONS TURD POLISHING. COULD YOU EXPLAIN THAT A BIT.
THANKS, JOHN
MELBOURNE, AUSTRALIA

HI JOHN, YOUR RESULTS SOUND TYPICAL. THE POWER OF THE MIND IS AN IMPORTANT CONCEPT FOR PEOPLE TO LEARN. HOWEVER, IT IS ONLY USING THE POWER OF THE MIND TO CHOOSE FORGIVENESS THAT REALLY MAKES ANY DIFFERENCE. THE SCRIPT IS WRITTEN, THE ONLY CHOICE AT ANY GIVEN MOMENT IS BETWEEN A LONGER OR SHORTER SCRIPT. MANIFESTING INTENTIONS HAS TO DO WITH THE LAW OF ATTRACTION. LIKE ATTRACTS LIKE. IF YOU ARE LIKE A POLISHED TURD, YOU'LL ATTRACT POLISHED TURDS. IF YOU ARE LIKE GOD (GUILTLESS), YOU'LL ATTRACT GOD. THE BEST THING TO DO WITH A TURD IS TO FLUSH IT. MAKING A BETTER DREAM IS FUTILE BECAUSE ALL SUCCESSES IN DREAMS ARE ONLY TEMPORARY. INSTEAD, YOU WANT TO WAKE UP, AND YOU DO THAT THROUGH FORGIVENESS. READ CHAPTER 7/9 SEVERAL TIMES.
SUBVERSIVELY, ALEX

DEAR ALEX,
I WISH YOU WOULD MAKE MORE COMICS FOR ME TO BUY. I JUST CAN'T GET ENOUGH. I'LL BUY AT LEAST TWO OF EVERY COMIC YOU MAKE, ONE FOR READING AND ONE FOR COLLECTING. DO YOU LIKE HORSES? I RECENTLY BOUGHT A HORSE. HIS NAME IS EVAN. HE LOVES YOUR COMICS TOO!
YOUR FAN, KYLE
BLACK FOREST, CO

WELL, YOU ARE DOING THE RIGHT THING. THE MORE COMICS PEOPLE BUY, THE MORE INCLINED I'LL BE TO MAKE MORE. EVAN SOUNDS LIKE A NICE HORSE.
WITH GRATITUDE, ALEX

DEAR ALEX,
YOU SHOULD COME TO RIO DE JANEIRO. I CAN SPEAK ENGLISH AND PORTUGUESE, SO I COULD BE YOUR TRANSLATOR. I AM PETITIONING THAT THE GIANT STATUE OF CHRIST THE REDEEMER BE TORN DOWN AN REPLACED WITH A STATUE OF YOUR RENDITION OF THE HOLY SPIRIT (ESPIRITO SANTO). WHAT DO YOU THINK?
SINCERELY, YASMIN
RIO DE JANEIRO, BRASIL

JUST BUY ME A PLANE TICKET, GIVE ME A PLACE TO STAY, FEED ME, AND DRIVE ME AROUND AND I'LL COME TO RIO WHENEVER YOU WANT. BUT WHEN I'M THERE, I'D LIKE TO SEE THE CHRIST THE REDEEMER STATUE. SO, DON'T TEAR IT DOWN YET. I LIKE THAT HE ISN'T HANGING ON A CROSS. LIKE ALL THINGS IN THIS DREAM, THAT STATUE WILL EVENTUALLY CRUMBLE. SO, AT THAT POINT IN TIME, I'LL BE ALL FOR YOUR PETITION.
ARTISTICALLY, ALEX

HI ALEX,
HOW COME YOU KEEP ON TAKING YOUR JACKET ON AND OFF THROUGHOUT THE BOOK?
MISTY
SEATTLE, WA

WELL, THAT IS BECAUSE IT KEPT GETTING WARM AND THEN COOL AND THEN WARM AGAIN WHILE I WAS MAKING THE BOOK. SO, I JUST MADE MY DRAWINGS BASED ON WHATEVER I WAS WEARING WHILE DRAWING.
COMFORTABLY, ALEX

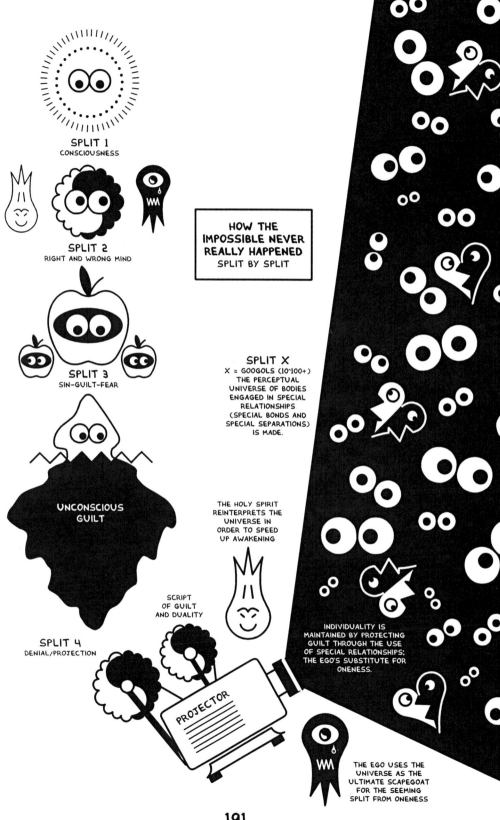

SPLIT 1
CONSCIOUSNESS

SPLIT 2
RIGHT AND WRONG MIND

SPLIT 3
SIN-GUILT-FEAR

UNCONSCIOUS
GUILT

SPLIT 4
DENIAL/PROJECTION

SCRIPT
OF GUILT
AND DUALITY

PROJECTOR

HOW THE
IMPOSSIBLE NEVER
REALLY HAPPENED
SPLIT BY SPLIT

SPLIT X
X = GOOGOLS (10^100+)
THE PERCEPTUAL
UNIVERSE OF BODIES
ENGAGED IN SPECIAL
RELATIONSHIPS
(SPECIAL BONDS AND
SPECIAL SEPARATIONS)
IS MADE.

THE HOLY SPIRIT
REINTERPRETS THE
UNIVERSE IN
ORDER TO SPEED
UP AWAKENING

INDIVIDUALITY IS
MAINTAINED BY PROJECTING
GUILT THROUGH THE USE
OF SPECIAL RELATIONSHIPS:
THE EGO'S SUBSTITUTE FOR
ONENESS.

THE EGO USES THE
UNIVERSE AS THE
ULTIMATE SCAPEGOAT
FOR THE SEEMING
SPLIT FROM ONENESS

191

NOTES

NOTES

VISIT ONLINE
WWW.ALEXANDERMARCHAND.COM

EXTRAS
NEWS
COMICS
MERCHANDISE
APPAREL
ORIGINAL ART
AND MORE

CPSIA information can be obtained at www.ICGtesting.com
Printed in the USA
BVOW042214140812

297905BV00005B/8/P

9 780982 923009